FOCUSED PASSION

Become Better, Faster, Smarter *and* Happier
With Far Less Stress *and* Much More Passion!

Steven Snyder

The Larry Czerwonka Company, LLC
Hilo, Hawai‘i

First Edition — June 2014

Published by: The Larry Czerwonka Company, LLC
http://thelarryczerwonkacompany.com

Printed in the United States of America

ISBN: 0692228683
ISBN-13: 978-0692228685

To Michael Benner, with whom I learned about the mind, and to Teresa Allred, with whom I learned about the heart.

Contents

Contents

Introduction (The Philosophy)

There is a New You that you can Breakthrough to.

For each and every individual—hidden behind their doubt, fear, worry, and confusion; enfolded within their role playing and people-pleasing persona—there is an Authentic Higher Self. This wonderful, wise and powerful New You is the sum total of your unique gifts, talents, abilities, and multiple intelligences as understood from a "higher perspective." This is your true and unique identity—the doorway to personal and professional mastery, to purpose and passion in your life, right here, right now.

The Alpha State, the state of Focused Passion is the way to get there.

There is a special state of mind and heart called the Alpha Brainwave State. It is also called the zone, or the flow. It is the state of Focused Passion. It's a tool that allows you to break through all of your blocks and resistances, doubts and fears, and access the amazing gifts, talents, abilities of the Authentic Higher Self—the New You that you are breaking through to.

Some Benefits of the Focused Passion State:

1. Mental and emotional rehearsal leads to states of peak performance.
2. Focused concentration brings about enhanced memory and accelerated learning.
3. Releasing stress helps to create optimum health and wellness.
4. Greater access to intuition results in higher creative intelligence.
5. Emotional Management replaces knee jerk reactions with well reasoned responses.

6. Imagination, insight, and ingenuity, enhances problem solving and innovation.

7. Reprogramming attitudes and habits, unlocks positive talents, gifts, and abilities.

Focused Passion is a state of two minds working together; the thinking mind and the feeling mind. One mind is the Adult, Conscious thought based BrainMind. It's the one you are usually aware of while walking around during the day. It is a mind of words, sounds, and pictures, ruled by deductive reasoning, logic, and will power. The other mind, the Subconscious feeling based HeartMind, is the one that holds your memories, runs the auto-pilot systems of your body, and dreams at night. It is a mind of emotion and sensation, ruled by imagination and feelings and capable of conceptual (big picture) understanding. The Conscious BrainMind uses analysis and deduction to solve problems. It uses a process of elimination, take-apart kind of thinking. As we look at the menu with our BrainMind, we decide by process of elimination, I don't want breakfast, and I don't want desert, I think I'll have a sandwich. But I don't want roast beef, and I don't want corned beef, and I don't want grilled cheese, I think I'll have turkey.

Your HeartMind is not deductive but rather inductive. It possesses all the information that you have ever known about yourself, about food, and about restaurants. This mind of imagination would push the menu aside and tune into feelings such as, "what am I in the mood for?" "What do I feel like?" "What would taste delicious right now?" HeartMind might even ask for chicken and waffles.

The BrainMind assembles a jig-saw puzzle by eliminating the pieces that don't fit and choosing the one that does. This HeartMind, upon seeing a partially assembled jigsaw puzzle, can go beyond what it knows, and realize that the fully assembled picture will be of a ship. The BrainMind uses deductive logic, or *take apart* thinking. The HeartMind uses inductive logic, or *put together* thinking.

There is a wonderful reason that explains why human beings have developed two different minds. It is because, in the whole world, there are truly only two problems. That's always been a comforting thought, only two problems in the whole world. One problem is, we know what we want, but we don't know how to get it, and the other problem is, "we don't know what we want."

The Conscious BrainMind has developed many rational methods to deduce the solution to the problem of "you know what you want, but you don't know how to get it." If you know that what you want, you can keep narrowing down the choices on the menu of ways to get it until you decide which one to pursue.

However if you don't know what you want, then you don't know where to go to see if there are any choices to choose from. Logic is useless as what you want has nothing to do with logic. What you want, or what your heart desires, is not a logical but rather an emotional question. It is a feeling. With deductive logic you could solve the problem of what you *think* you are *supposed* to want, by selecting from among those things other people have suggested. But not the problem of what do you really want, because there is no logical menu to choose from.

> "I understand," said the BrainMind. "You take the pieces, like our thoughts, feelings, knowledge, and wisdom, and assemble them into the whole, our desired outcome. Then I take that desired outcome and break it down to the individual pieces such as the steps we need to take to achieve it. First we go to you to help decide what we want. Then we come back to me to help figure out, step by step, how to get it."
>
> "Right," said HeartMind. "You focus on the things to do, and I empower us to make them true."

Determining what you feel you truly want calls for something from the HeartMind like imagination, inspiration, insight, intuition, or illumination, not deductive logic. When you have no idea what you want you can not use deduction or process of elimination. You must use inductive, or *put together* thinking. However, sometimes the way we answer the question "What do I want," comes purely through your emotions. You just want it. You have an intuition that it would be good. You imagine that it would make you feel better. However the question, "what do I want," could have so many possible answers, a better question to ask is, "what do I want THE MOST!"

When we were newly born, we are inherently HeartMind. We have no logic, will power, or deductive ability. For example, at first there was no preconceived method for sitting up. We creatively experimented with many different methods. Due to our passion for achievement, it wasn't long before we began to use everything available to aid us in our endeavors. We began to repeat aspects of those sitting up methods that seemed to work. Ultimately we discover a "right combination" that creates the desired result. There are a lot of different movements that we could do that could lead to sitting up. We find those right combinations of movements that are easier than the others until we get a right combination that works pretty good. We then do this one over and over again, and before long it is a habit. We can then relegate sitting up to the automatic pilot of HeartMind and put our attention on other things.

Early childhood is made up to a great extent of imagining, daydreaming and pretending. Our creativity flourishes in a structure where there are so few rules, and where it is relatively okay to be wrong. Curiosity is the driving force, and fascination is the reward for the experience. At a time when our creativity and problem solving skills are peaking, we run head on into a very sobering experience for both BrainMind and HeartMind called school.

"School," said BrainMind, "it seems to me, was more directed toward Brain than Heart. But it was only when Heart got involved, only when we got interested, that we actually learned anything."

"True," said HeartMind, "when I was interested it was easy to learn, for that was where my Heart would turn. When I was bored then I would go away, and that's where I spent many a day. For the most part I found school for me, was boredom, with jolts of high anxiety."

The Industrial Age, process of schooling children utilized a system that blocked much of their imagination and creativity. Essentially, the original point of schooling was preparing children for assembly line jobs. We took all of the kids of the same age, put them in the same room, and taught them how to do the same things, in the same way, at the same time. To make them all the same. Ideally they would all graduate at the same age with the same skills, and the same information base, working at the same speed as each other. It's like a school of fish. To be in the school, fish have to swim the same way as all of the other fish do. If they are different, and they swim off by themselves, they are not in the school anymore.

School was designed to meet the needs of the Industrial Age society that existed when it was instituted, and at the time what we needed was millions of assembly line factory workers. People who could follow directions and do repetitive tasks at the same speed as everyone around them. School was perfect for creating students to meet the needs of an assembly line technology, where being the same (conformity) is more effective than being different (creativity).

The result of schooling for many, has been the acceptance of averageness, blocking many members of our society from experiencing the creativity (the specialness and uniqueness) that is their birthright. The Information Age has remarkably different needs than the Industrial Age had. We have moved from the factories to the offices. We have moved from a work culture where most everyone did much the same job, to a work culture with much more diversity. Assembly line jobs are handled more and more by robots and computer assisted engineering, while humans are freed up to do jobs where they must solve problems and creatively think. The primary thinking skills that one needs in our modern day culture is knowing how to make things up, and how to figure things out; innovation and problem solving.

An important function of the state of Focused Passion is that it allows us access to both of our minds at the same time. This allows the minds to work most effectively with the kind of effectiveness that will be needed to meet the needs of a rapidly changing corporate technology and an even more rapidly changing marketplace.

LEARNING PASSION

What do we do with this system of schooling
That seems to grow more obsolete
Just who in the world do we think we are fooling
The system is dead on its feet
Designed for times that were not like these
And different locks need different keys
The system's not working as everyone sees
With eyes to the future we turn
Make it change so our children can learn

The children no longer require a school
To teach them to memorize stuff
We now have computers, a wonderful tool
That can memorize more than enough
Designed for times that were not like these
Training worker bees for factories
But now we have robots that do as we please
With eyes to the future we turn
Make it change so our children can learn
We don't need a system that makes us the same
But instead treats us all as unique
No need to recall every date, every name
But instead how to learn, think and seek
Designed for times that are not like these
We need to see forests and not just the trees
Our children's minds can learn with ease
If we just let the old system go
Make it change so our children can grow

School comes to an end, education survived
Where students can learn what they choose
In the twenty first century, passion's revived
Learning passion's a tool that they use
Creatively think, and do it with ease
Problems become opportunities seized
Passion sets in and the boredom it flees
With eyes to the future we turn
It's reborn, so our children can learn

Using Focused Passion allows us to think beyond the boundaries of what is known. You make use of the Alpha Brainwave State, the particular brainwaves that provide access to both Conscious BrainMind and Subconscious HeartMind which allows for the state of Focused Passion with its enhanced creativity and problem solving skills.

> "I love problem solving." said BrainMind. "I love the challenge of making things better."
> "I too love the challenge that problem solving brings, because I love making things better and making better things," said HeartMind.

Everyone can be assisted in becoming accelerated learners with the AlphaLearning System of Focused Passion. Learning, in the Alpha Brainwave State, to focus concentration, reduce stress and tension, access greater creative intelligence, and enhance reading, thinking, and memory skills, makes anyone more effective and productive.

> "When I speak to you," said BrainMind, "no matter what I say, PASSION amplifies the signal. PASSION is truly the language that you best understand."

"YES, YES, YES," said HeartMind. "You DO see. PASSION is the key to communicate with me. We are the two of us, both energy, I'm one side of you, and you're one side of me."

The Life Force

To have an understanding of the mind we must start with the basics, matter and energy. The body is matter. What is not matter, what animates the matter is energy. In India they call it Kundalini, in China it is called *Chi*, in Japan it's *Ki*, in French it is *Elan Vital*, in Hindi it is *Ru*, in Hebrew it is *Ruach*, on Hawai'i it's called *Mana*, and in New Orleans it's called *Mojo*. The Chinese translate *Chi*, into English as Life Force. The Life Force energy is the energy that is life itself. The Life Force flows through human beings in three ways. It has three manifestations, three jobs to do.

1. **The Life Force flows through our physical bodies as pain control and healing.** Without our needing to have the slightest idea how it works, (even doctors don't fully understand how it works), our bodies know exactly how to heal themselves. The mandate is "fix and make better." If the skin gets cut, our body will not only fix the cut, but it will replace the skin with scar tissue, which is stronger than skin and less likely to be re-cut. If we break a bone, the body repairs it stronger than it was before—less likely to be re-broken. If we get mumps, or measles, or chicken pox, or bodies will heal with an added resistance to the disease. We build up immunities and are stronger than we were before. Whether dealing with injury or disease, the life force as it flows through the focused brain seeks to fix the body and make it better.

2. **The Life Force flows through our minds as intelligence and creativity.** Other names might include imagination,

intuition, inspiration, revelation, and illumination. The highest form of intelligence is the "ah ha" experience. Those times when the light bulb goes off over your head, and you come up with a brilliant solution or an absolutely brilliant idea. This is the product of a focused brain. The lowest form of intelligence comes doing rote memorization and repetitive tasks.

3. **The Life Force flows through our spirit as passion, self-confidence, and love.** Love is the most common name, but it can also be called peace of mind, feelings of well being, and the inner sense of safety and security. These are also manifestations of the life force in a focused brain. We get to experience excellent health, happiness, passion, and success as a result of allowing the life force to flow unimpeded through the human spirit.

Healing, intelligence, and love are all the same thing. They are all the life force. This is why hateful people are often sick and stupid. If you block your life force by blocking your love, you also block your intelligence and healing. It is all one force.

Brainwave States

This Life Force is science. You can measure it on a machine. The machine called the electroencephalograph or EEG, and what it measures is brain wave activity. Brainwaves are a measurement of the Life Force. It is rather crude measurement, but it has been the best that science can do so far.

A flat EEG, registering no Life Force, is how we currently determine death. It used to be you were determined to be dead when your heart stopped beating, but sometimes we can get the heart going again. You're considered dead when the EEG, doesn't show any brain wave activity. Brain wave activity is one crude measurement of the Life Force.

Brainwave activity has been divided by scientists into four categories, or Brainwave States. They call them Delta, Theta, Alpha and Beta. So what you are about to learn is Delta, Theta, Alpha, Beta, Data.

Delta is a state that is anything above zero to four cycles per second on the electroencephalograph or EEG. We have a name for it, we call it deep sleep. Cycles per second or hertz is the way we measure brainwave activity and also other forces of energy as well. For example, radio waves are transmitted through the airways in cycles per second. FM radio waves are measured in millions of cycles per second. If I tune it to 95.5 on the FM dial, I'm picking up a frequency being broadcast at 95,500,000 cycles per second. If I tune to the AM dial, which is a lower frequency dial, then I'm tuning in to say 640 on the AM dial, I'm tuning into 640,000 cycles per second. Audible sound is anything from about 60 cycles per second to about 20,000 cycles per second.

What we bounce off satellites can be gigahertz, or billions of cycles per second. But of all the energy in the universe, light, heat, color, sound, x-rays, microwaves; human brainwaves are the lowest frequency of them all.

Brain waves are the only form of energy where the frequency begins at zero. We call this birth and death. Actually it is the birth of brain wave activity, which begins late in the second trimester of pregnancy and continues until we die.

Hopefully none of us will experience the state above zero but below a half a cycle per second, this is comatose or coma. But what all of us experience virtually every day is the state that starts at a half a cycle per second and goes up to for cycles per second, the state that we call deep sleep. Sleep is a fantastic thing. The most surprising thing about sleep is, nobody has any idea what happens when they were there, and yet everybody wants to go back. It's like, I know it was good, I don't remember a thing about it, but I know it must have been good.

For adults, there are at least two primary reasons we sleep: One of them is to heal the body, and the other is to regulate brain chemistry. Most healthy uninjured adults require seven or eight hours of sleep, but we all need at least eight hours of rest. The problem is that many people have no idea how to rest unless they are sleeping. These hyper Type A Personalities have only two speeds FULL and OFF. These people need at least eight hours of sleep as they never get any other rest. With enough effective rest, some can do well with less sleep.

As we move up from Delta, the deep-sleep state, toward awake we move into Theta. Theta is a range from about 4 *to* 7 cycles per second on the EEG. This is a state we still consider being asleep, but is quite different from deep sleep. Theta is where we dream.

Dreams are fascinating because they can tell us about the subconscious part of us that we aren't normally in touch with.

Theta includes the state of dreaming, but that's not quite all. Theta is something like an iceberg, with most of it below the level of consciousness with a tip of the iceberg floating above. There is this half awake/half asleep place, where you are dreaming, but you know that you are dreaming while you are dreaming it. Where you are having a lucid dream.

We have this very powerful trance-like state in between awake and asleep. This is the place that the Maharishis, Yogis, Fakirs, and Zen Masters all go to when they do those wondrous things they do. Like walking on burning hot coals or laying on beds of sharp nails. In this half awake/half asleep, "tip of the iceberg" part of the Theta State, we have the potential to exert tremendous control over our physical bodies. Theta, however, takes a long time to master. We're talking about deep trance meditation where you have to sit and quiet your mind for twenty or thirty minutes every morning and twenty or thirty minutes every evening, with an investment of months and months for gifted naturals and years for most people, to be able to get significant results. Ultimately meditation is a powerful thing to do, but in many people's busy lives, it's pretty inconvenient. If we lived in a cave in Tibet or a mountaintop in the Andes, this would be easier, but for many their lives are so busy, it's challenging to find the time to invest twenty minutes every morning and twenty minutes every evening and then have to wait months or even years for the rewards.

The technique that you are about to learn doesn't take twenty minutes. In fact, the technique that you are about to learn takes twenty seconds. Now in twenty seconds you can't master the Theta State, but what you can master is Alpha, the state of total focused concentration on one thing. While it's hard to find twenty minutes to do Theta, it is easy to find twenty seconds to do Alpha. Every time you get in the car before you turn the key you've got twenty seconds, even if you are late, in fact, especially if you are late, that's when you most need Alpha. Every time you go to the bathroom or when you hang up the phone or before you have to do the next thing. You have time before you start anything and time when you finish, to create those twenty seconds. There are a lot of opportunities in the course of your day, and you don't even have to take out your iPhone and schedule it in.

It's quite easy to get into Alpha. Any time you daydream you go to Alpha. Any time you remember something or fantasize about something, that's Alpha. In fact, the scientific name of the Alpha Brainwave State, with your eyes open, is called staring. Any time you're staring at something or staring at nothing that's Alpha. We go in and out of Alpha all day long, it's the easiest thing in the world to do. As a matter of fact, two of our favorite pastimes happen in the Alpha State, watching television and spacing out. It is remarkably easy to get into Alpha, but the problem is that most people use Alpha primarily, if not exclusively to "space out." You're about to learn how to use that state to in addition, "space in."

Traditionally brainwave activity is divided into four levels as measured on an EEG.

Level	Cycles Per Second	Description
Beta	14 *to* 40	Divided Attention/Scattered/Panic
Alpha	7 *to* 14	Daydreaming/Focus
Theta	4 *to* 7	Dreaming/Trance
Delta	+0 *to* -4	Comatose/Deep Sleep

(Recently scientists have discovered another brainwave state above 40 cycles they call the Gamma State. While little is known about Gamma, it seems to be associated with bursts of insight and high level information processing.)

Beta: This is the brainwave state that we associate with being awake. It can be categorized by divided attention. Conversation usually takes place in the lower beta range. Confusion, anxiety, and terror occur in the higher beta range.

Alpha: This is the state of focused concentration and hyper-suggestibility experienced in daydreaming, watching television, and listening to music; as well as in states of light hypnosis and meditation. Artists, athletes, musicians and others who achieve greatness also experience it.

Theta: This state includes the sleep dreams and that state in between awake and asleep when we are dreaming and know that we are dreaming at the same time. Deep hypnosis and trance meditation is part of the Theta State.

Delta: This is the deep sleep state. In this state of healing and regeneration, the metabolic rate slows and our bodies repair themselves. Our conscious mind is turned off and there is no thinking or dreaming taking place. The physical body is totally at rest.

The lowest range of brainwave activity, the Delta Brainwave State, goes from comatose states up through ordinary sleep. The Theta State begins with dream sleep and takes us up through the half awake state of deep trance. The Alpha Brainwave State begins when we are barely awake and goes up through focused peak performance states. Beta is the state that begins with simple divided attention and goes all the way up through panic, anxiety, confusion, and terror.

In the Alpha Brainwave State, the Conscious BrainMind (the mind of logic and reasoning), and the Subconscious HeartMind (the mind of creativity and imagination) work together in harmony. As we focus our concentration in the Alpha Brainwave State, certain neurological pathways in the brain become stimulated, allowing greater electro-chemical connections between our conscious and our subconscious minds. With the filter (the reticular activating system) open, we have access to far more of our creative intelligence. Everything becomes easier to learn.

In today's complex world, we spend a lot of time in the Beta Brainwave State, where our attention is divided when we are thinking about several ideas at the same time. The busier our lives get, the more time we tend to spend in Beta. Sometimes it is appropriate for us to be in the Beta State. There are many occasions in our daily lives, such as driving, caring for children, or meeting important deadlines, that involve multi-tasking, and demand divided or split attention.

There are; however, many more occasions that benefit from the focused concentration and undivided intensity of the Alpha Brainwave State. It is the athlete's peak performance state and the inventor's creativity. It is the surgeon's focus and the stamp collector's concentration. It is every child's state of fascination, wonder and awe.

The Alpha Brainwave State is the state for greatness at any endeavor because only in Alpha can we focus concentration, and thus accomplish whatever we most desire. Beta is a stressful state. The more time we spend feeling anxious, nervous, frightened, or confused, the harder it is on our minds and our bodies.

When we get stressed, or endangered, we utilize the primitive portion of our brain for our survival. We gain access to strength and speed. This is best known as "the fight or flight syndrome." At the same time; however, we tend to lose access to the more evolved parts of our brain; and to our intelligence, creativity, and recall. In the Beta State, we can get fast and strong, but also stupid and forgetful.

We are much smarter in Alpha. We can quickly master a powerful technique to put ourselves into the Alpha State anytime we choose, in less than twenty seconds. In Alpha, we amplify interest in any subject, and focus both our conscious and subconscious minds on enjoying the process of understanding and learning. We can read even the most technical of material several times faster than we ever could have before while significantly improving our comprehension, retention, and recall. In addition to enhanced logic and reasoning skills, we have access to our imagination, intuition, inspiration, and ingenuity as well. AlphaLearners have learned to control their own brainwave activity. The connection between peak performance and accelerated learning, is the effective use of Focused Passion while in the Alpha Brainwave State.

"So Delta and Theta, sleep and dreaming, are mostly for you," said BrainMind, "and Beta, divided attention and multi-tasking, is for me. The Alpha State is where we can both play together."

"Alpha," said HeartMind, "is powerful and fun. Alpha is the state where we both can be as one."

Controlling your own brainwave activity and bringing yourself into Alpha allows you gain access and bring passion to both your logical deductive intelligence, and also the emotional creative intelligence that is found in the mind that dreams at night. We are in each of the four brainwave states most every day.

Going toward sleep is what brings our brainwave activity down; waking up brings it back up. It happens automatically, but it can be controlled intentionally. Developing this conscious control is a primary tool of AlphaLearners.

There are many techniques for lowering brainwave activity from, yoga, the martial arts, self-hypnosis, meditation, biofeedback, creative visualization, and practical daydreaming. It is best, however, to have one familiar technique that allows you instant access to the Alpha Brainwave State.

Here is a Quick Way to Get Into Alpha

1. Close your eyes. Alpha can be easily reached with eyes open as in watching television or in daydreaming, or staring off into space. However, closing your eyes helps cut out many of the more obvious distractions. About 86% of all sensory input comes in through the eyes. Just closing your eyes, all by itself, is often enough to create the Alpha State.

2. Take a slow deep breath and focus on your heart. (Deep breathing is the most basic technique known to begin a process of relaxing the mind/body into the Alpha Brainwave State.) Inhale slowly, a little beyond the point where you usually would stop, in order to fill up your lungs and expand the area around your heart. Hold the breath for a moment or two, focusing on the feelings of self confidence and self esteem, then slowly release the breath.

3. Imagine yourself in a peaceful place, a calm, serene, safe, and tranquil place of perfect peace. It could be a place from memory or fantasy or some of each, as long as it's a peaceful place and it relaxes you. You might see brilliant colors or perhaps you'll hear peaceful sounds. You can feel like there is beauty all around you and experience the feeling of love surrounding you there. Imagine you can smell the sweet fragrances of nature and that you can taste the freshness of the air. As you imagine yourself in this peaceful place, just pretend that it is real and that you are actually there. Now bookmark this place so

you can return any time you choose. Your mind, your amazing mind is such a powerful tool for you to use.

4. Focus on any area of your life that you choose. You could concentrate on your career, your relationships, your health, or your prosperity. If you don't know where to begin, then you begin, with the question, "What do I want the most?"

Tune in to yourself and just see what's in there, or listen to yourself and hear what's in there, or get in touch with yourself and feel what's in there. Choose the area of your life where you would like to focus first. Whenever you don't know what to do, your first task is always to determine the answer to that exact question, "what do I want?" If you already know what you want, then ask yourself "what do I do to get it?" . . . then imagine yourself doing it. After you have chosen an area where you want to begin your work, you next determine what you would like to discover or develop. Choose a goal, but realize that the purpose of a goal is not to achieve it, but rather to give you a direction to take your next step.

You can begin to pursue a goal and then change your mind along the way. The point is to get moving. Once you have chosen a goal (a potential destination), imagine that you have successfully achieved your goal and get in touch with just how wonderful it feels to have done so. See it or pretend to see it. If it isn't easy to visualize it, that is seeing pictures with your mind's eye, simply imagine what it would look like if you could see it. If you imagine an umbrella, whether you see it or not, you know if it is opened or closed.

Amplify the intensity of these positive emotions and let them become the magnets that will draw you towards your self-discovery or your personal development. Decide your next step. Determine what is the first thing you have to do to get started.

You can make it a little thing, an easy thing, a baby step, something that you know you can do. The laws of physics state "an object in motion tends to stay in motion," take a baby step and get moving.

The Four Ps:
The Laws of Suggestion

All suggestions must be Positive.

The subconscious mind can only understand positive suggestions. It needs to be told what to do, rather than what not to do. "Don't think of rainbows" is the same as "Think of rainbows." Negative suggestions not only don't work, they waste a lot of time

All suggestions must be made in the Present tense.

The subconscious mind only understands **now**. Suggestions that are given for tomorrow or some unspecified future date will not become active. They will stay on hold until it is tomorrow or later. The problem is that it is never tomorrow, it is always today. It is never later, it is always now. Suggestions for a specific future time can be given effectively if you imagine that it is that future time **now** as you give the suggestion.

The power is increased by Persistence, Perseverance, or Practice.

As the subconscious mind does not understand time, imagining something for one minute or less can be the same as imagining it for twenty minutes. It is much more powerful to imagine something twenty times for a minute each time than once for twenty minutes.

How much power each suggestion has is based on Passion.

Emotion is the primary language of the subconscious mind. The words and pictures are the steering wheel, they set the direction, but emotion is the gas pedal. Emotion is the factor that determines how much power suggestions will have. The ultimate power of suggestion is determined by X number of repetitions at Y emotional amplitude.

> "Positive, Present, Practice, and Passion," said BrainMind. "Positive, Present, Practice and Passion, Positive, Present Practice and Passion. Positive, Present Practice and Passion."
>
> HeartMind said, "remembering these rules are easy for me, the laws all start with the letter **P**."

There are two basic kinds of Focused Passion Alpha techniques. In one style, you use the BrainMind to listen to the HeartMind. Either ask questions and wait for answers, or just listen. This is called introspection, reflection, or mindfulness and it leads to Self Discovery. In the other style, a more active style, you use the BrainMind to program the HeartMind with the four Ps. This is a form of Personal Development. Listening, we can pick and choose the thoughts by which we would like to continue to be influenced, and then reinforce them. We can say YES to the good thoughts. We can release negative thoughts by simply taking a deep breath and thinking, "I'm sure glad I got that thought out of my system!" Doing this takes away the power from negative thoughts rendering them inert and impotent. It is only the thoughts and feelings that we agree with that have the power to change us. When we think about getting up from where we are sitting, that thought has to be agreed with to become active. If we had that thought (I'm going to get up) and decided no; then we wouldn't get up. The thought by itself does not produce the change. If you say no, and release the thought, you take away its power. Only those thoughts that we agree with have power. Saying no and taking a deep breath, releases the suggestion from your mind.

If you say yes to the good thoughts, and no to the bad ones, every thought that you think will help you grow and increase your level of self-esteem. Saying yes to the good thoughts and no to the bad thoughts is a great way to change your mind. This is the key to becoming less pessimistic and more optimistic every single day. We estimate we have between 12,000 and 60,000 thoughts each day, many of them conscious, but most below our level of consciousness. The act of tuning into the subconscious with all of our attention lets the mind know that the information is important, and it acts upon that information with greater power.

"So I get to the Alpha Brainwave State," said BrainMind, "and I listen to thoughts, and I say yes to the good ones and no to the bad ones, to release the bad ones and empower the good ones."

"If you say no, and then release, bad thoughts will lessen and might even cease. Say yes to good thoughts and focus in that fashion, then I, HeartMind, will provide us with all the Passion."

Unlocking the Power of "I"

I: The essential self, the center of consciousness,
that part that is self-aware.

Intelligence: Capacity for reasoning, understanding, and other forms of mental activity.

Imagination: The action of forming mental images or concepts of what is not actually present.

Induction: Reasoning where the conclusion does not necessarily follow from the premises.

Intuition: Direct perception of the truth, independent of any reasoning process.

Invention: The act or instance of producing or creating by the exercise of the imagination.

Inspiration: An animating, quickening, or exalting, thought, action or influence.

Insight: Penetrating mental vision or discernment, faculty for seeing underlying truth.

Illumination: Intellectual or spiritual enlightenment. To light up, to throw light on.

Introspection: Observation or examination of one's own mental and emotional state.

Intension: Exertion of the mind. Determination, intensity to a high degree.

Ideation: The process of forming ideas or images in the mind.

Improvisation: Composing extemporaneously, creating at the spur of the moment.

Interest: That which draws attention, concern, curiosity, or involvement.

Innovation: Something new or different introduced. Creating with new outcomes.

Instigation: To urge, provoke, or incite, some action or course.

Intention: One's attitude toward the effects of one's actions or conduct. One's purpose.

Initiation: To introduce into the knowledge, some art or subject.

Investigation: To make an inquiry or examination of the particulars, in an attempt to learn.

Initiative: Readiness and ability to take a leading action. One's personal enterprise.

Implementation: To fulfill, perform, or carry out, with a definite plan or procedure.

Ingenuity: Skill or cleverness in planning or inventing.

The way we answer the question "What do you want" isn't by using any kind of logic at all. . . . Sometimes your subconscious mind comes to the answer purely through your emotions. You just want it. You have an intuition that it would feel good. You imagine that it would make you happy. All of our earliest problems were solved this way. When we were newly born, we are totally subconscious. We have no logic, and just about all there is, is creativity.

Each time we would awaken from one of our frequent sleeps, we had no plans, we didn't know what we were supposed to do. There was nothing logical to base it on. There were no habits, no automatic responses beyond our survival needs. We would make it up as we went along. We saw something moving, or brightly colored, and our attention was instantly drawn to it. We created a whole universe inside of this one specific thing existing for the entire duration of our short attention spans.

An important function of the Alpha State the state of Focused Passion is that it allows us access to both of our minds at the same time. This allows the minds to most effectively think. The kind of thinking that will be needed to meet the needs of a rapidly changing corporate technology and an even more rapidly changing marketplace. Using the Alpha Brainwave State allows us to think beyond the boundaries of what is known. With Focused passion, you make use of the particular brainwaves that provides access to both conscious and

22

subconscious minds and allows for enhanced creativity and problem solving skills.

As we leave the Industrial Age, there is a need to develop different skills. In this Information Age, the two most valuable skills become making things up and figuring things out. In the past, many people had very similar jobs—working in factories on the assembly line. In the future, specialization is becoming more and more prevalent; and, in the office, everyone is doing something different. We can no longer depend on the same old answers because we are creating brand new problems.

How we experience our problems is a more significant factor in our happiness than are the specific problems that we experience. Life is not about becoming free of problems, rather it is about becoming a better and better problem solver. Instead of complaining and worrying, we can learn to see our problems as creative opportunities that give us the chance to grow and improve. We can take on our problems as puzzles to be solved, or as challenges to be enthusiastically faced.

When we get into stressful beta states, we move into fight or flight syndrome, where the only problem we are prepared to solve is survival. The filter or reticular activating system between the conscious and subconscious minds closes down, denying us access to memory and creativity. By utilizing the alpha state you get in touch with your problem solving capabilities. With the filter open, you can use your imagination to go beyond what you know into all that could be.

Often it is difficult to solve our problems because we can't clearly see the problem for what it truly is. This is the "you can't see the forest for the trees" syndrome. We get caught up in the emotions and sometimes seem to blow the problem all out of proportion. Sometimes it serves to take an alternate perception and see the problem in a different way. Step outside of the problem, and change your perception, and the problem seems to change.

You could imagine that the problem belongs to someone else. If this were true, what kind of advice would you give them? What would you say that their first step could be? How would you help to motivate them and get them going? What resources would you suggest they utilize? How can you help them be confident of their process and their ultimate success?

You could pretend that the problem is already solved. Think backwards from the solution back to the first step. Imagine that you are remembering how you did it. Where were you when you figured it out, and what were you doing? Realize how delightful it feels to have it solved. Be proud of yourself. Sometimes we can solve a problem, simply by realizing that it is not actually a problem at all. Many problems can be seen in a positive light, as creative opportunities to exercise our minds and our talents to create some positive change. For every problem, there are solutions. Some are better than others.

One of the most limiting forms of thinking is to assume that there is only one right answer to your problem. This rigid and restrictive thinking process comes from the rigid and restrictive experience of school. One right answer and everything else is *wrong*. We must break out of that mold in order to be truly effective problem solvers.

If you relax your mind, and use your imagination and your creativity, you will find unlimited resources at your disposal. Almost all of the great problems that have ever been solved or inventions invented have had their solutions begin in some woman's or some man's daydream. It is the daydream-like Alpha State where most great ideas are born. One little clue or creative idea is all that it takes to begin solving the most perplexing problems.

Alpha is a powerful tool to get in touch with your memory and imagination. It is a superb technique to improve your capacity for problem solving and to enhance your creativity. You can program your mind to help you solve your problems. You can program your mind to open up to a very powerful channel of creative energy, enhance your insight, intuition, and inspiration, and inspire your mind into feats of genius. You can empower your conscious and subconscious minds together to create almost any outcome you choose.

An important function of the Alpha State is to foster the initiative to think beyond the boundaries of what is. The purpose is to promote the kind of thinking that will be needed to meet the needs of a rapidly changing corporate technology and an even more rapidly changing marketplace. In Alpha, you make use of those particular states of mind that provide access to the power of creativity.

As we said, life is not about becoming free of problems, rather it is about becoming a better problem solver. Instead of complaining and worrying, we can learn to see our problems as creative opportunities that give us the chance to grow and improve. We can take on our problems as puzzles to be solved, or as challenges to be overcome. When we get into stressful beta states, the filter or reticular activating system closes down, denying us access to memory and creativity. By utilizing the alpha state you get in touch with your problem solving capabilities. With the filter open, you can use your imagination to go beyond what you know into all that could be. Often it is difficult to solve problems because we can't clearly see the problem for what it truly is.

The secret to success is not only knowing what to use but also using what you know. Then comes using what you know over and over again with great passion. Persistence and passion are the keys.

Changing the way you read is a metaphor for life. With the same techniques, you can reprogram any habit, attitude, or behavior you choose. Remember, change can often bring up doubt and fear. Realize that if getting some assistance would be of service to you as you experience your changes, then you deserve it. With Alpha, you know you have the power to manage change, and knowing you can, will let you realize that you must.

Representational Systems

There are three primary styles that we use to think and to learn, to intake and process information. We use seeing (visual), hearing (auditory) and feeling (kinesthetic). The feeling or kinesthetic sense includes smell and taste, tactile and physical sensations, as well as emotions, and intuitions. Each of us uses all three of these systems, but we use them to differing degrees. Most of us tend to use one or two of the three more than the others. Some people use only one most of the time.

Visual: Those that are primarily visual tend to speak quickly, breathe shallowly, look upward for their information, and use phrases such as "I see what you mean," or "I get the picture." Visual people are faster paced and often more active than others tend to be.

Auditory: Auditory people tend to love the sound of their own voice. They breathe evenly, look to the side (toward their ears) for their information, and use phrases like "Sounds good to me," or "I hear you." They are usually even paced, and even-tempered, and are often excellent listeners.

Kinesthetic: Those people that are more kinesthetic tend to speak slower and seem to look down (into their bodies) for their information. They use phrases such as "I'm getting a feel for it," or "I can't quite get a handle on it." They move through life more deliberately and often have a better understanding of self than others do. It is sometimes difficult for kinesthetic people to express their feelings in a way others can understand.

Understanding your primary representational system will help you to better understand and more effectively re-program the habits that no longer serve you. Understanding the primary representational system of others can help lead you toward better communication skills. Listen to the words people use when they talk to you, to help you identify their system.

Some Key Words

Visual	Auditory	Kinesthetic
see	loud	feel
imagine	quiet	touch
visualize	listen	grasp
focus	hear	rub
bright	tonal	shake
clear	ringing	hot
colorful	harmony	cold
picture	sound	hurt
scan	squeaking	handle
look	whisper	press
shiny	shout	stub
dull	buzzing	push

Transformational Conversations

How to become Exceptional at having
Important Talks with Significant People

People engage in many levels of conversation. From having pleasant inconsequential small talk, to our most important communications, with the most significant people in our lives. It is those consequential talks that make the most difference that I call Transformational Conversations. It is most important to rehearse and experience these conversations in the Alpha State, the state of Focused Passion.

Conversations such as:
- Talking with your spouse about the best ways to parent.
- Talking with your partner about where the company could go.
- Talking with an employee about improving their performance.
- Talking with your kids about right and wrong, and yes and no.
- Use Focused Passion to manage stress and set up states of peak performance.
- Use Focused Passion to release negative patterns and create successful results.
- Develop Reflective Communication Skills to develop rapport and insure clarity.
- Use Alpha for building confidence, developing interest, and enhancing empathy.

We all have important conversations. Working to maximize their outcomes can be among our most rewarding experiences. These Transformational Conversations can be the crossroads, the turning points that determine our future. In circumstances such as these, exceptional focus, clarity, empathy, and understanding are essential.

These vital exchanges are the Olympic Events of our lives.

Tips for Transformational Conversations:

- Focus your attention and passion, to make conversations, truly peak performances.
- Tune in to your partner's process and content, to be in harmony with their message.
- Guide your partner into understanding your process, to promote communication.
- Program your mind to create, and to be prepared to receive, your desired outcomes.
- Converse in a state with access to creative genius, to handle the unexpected.
- Finish conversations, feeling like you did your best, and gave it your all!

Let Go And Prepare To Listen.

Alpha Exercise — Close your eyes . . . take a deep breath . . . imagine your peaceful place. Take about a minute and with each inhale say, "I am relaxed" (or similar words), and with each exhale say something like, "I am at peace." Feel yourself letting go of what you were doing and begin to unwind. Whenever you are ready, open your eyes.

Focus Your Brainmind And Heartmind On Your Conversation Partner.

Alpha Exercise — Close your eyes . . . take a deep breath . . . and again imagine your peaceful place. Begin to think about the person with whom you are going to be speaking. Become aware of the thoughts and feeling that come up for you. Notice these thoughts and feelings with no judgement or attachment to any of them. Next, recall (or imagine) a positive experience that you have shared with this person. Think of something about them that you appreciate. Whenever you are ready, you can open your eyes.

Focus Your BrainMind And HeartMind On The Upcoming Conversation.

Alpha Exercise — Close your eyes . . . take a deep breath . . . and again imagine your peaceful place.

Begin to think about your intention and your optimum outcome for the upcoming conversation. Imagine the process flowing smoothly, with excellent communication.

Take Responsibility For Conversational Success.

It is easier to change the way you think than it is to change the way they think.

Alpha Exercise — Close your eyes . . . take a deep breath . . . and again imagine your peaceful place. Imagine coming to the end of the conversation with the realization that you stayed focused on the conversation the entire time and that your optimum outcome has been achieved.

Effective Listening

"Women like silent men. They think they are listening." (Marcel Ackard)

"No man would listen to you talk if he didn't know it was his turn next." (Edward W. Howe)

Common Reasons For Not Listening

- I want to talk first, or I'm thinking of what I'm going to say.
- I'm not interested in the subject.
- I don't like the person I'm talking to or I don't like the way they speak.
- I'm concerned about other things.
- I don't have time for this right now.

- I don't want to hear what I think is coming.

Active Listening

- Begin with a positive attitude. Prevent emotions from side-tracking your reasoning.
- Keep checking on your level of concentration. Stay as patient as you can.
- Analyze what's being said. Ask questions for clarification.
- Separate the relevant from the irrelevant. Test your understanding of what you hear.
- Consider the implications. Positive or negative consequences.
- Where does it fall on the scale of true or false/good or bad advice?
- Anticipate but don't prejudge where a particular line of thought is leading.
- Repeat the central points in your own words.
- Listen with your eyes. "You can observe a lot by just watching." (Yogi Berra)
- Listen with your intuition. Pay careful attention to your inner voice.

Effective Speaking

- Determine your purpose and desired outcome.
- Create an outline either mental or written.
- Tell them what you are going to tell them, tell them, then tell them what you told them.
- Clear negative emotions.
- "When angry count to 10 . . . If very angry, count to 100." (Thomas Jefferson)
- Express yourself with emotion whenever appropriate.
- Add humor whenever appropriate.
- Get to the point quickly and continue to be concise.

- Always be truthful. Ask for what you want.
- Keep it as simple. Make it appropriate for the listener.
- Tune into the mood of the listener. Respect the other person's point of view.
- Watch your posture. Dress for the occasion.
- Vary your volume, inflection, and intonation. Explain abstract words and concepts.
- Use absolutes and generalities sparingly.
- Use gender neutral language. Illustrate with personal examples.
- Tell stories.

Ten Transformational Conversations

1. Hiring Conversations
   (Meeting / Exploring / Interviewing / Auditioning)
2. Information Conversations
   (Mentor / Learner / Questioning / Collaborating)
3. Decision Conversations
   (Negotiating / Goal Setting / Reaching Conclusions)
4. Empathy Conversations
   (Sharing Feelings / Emotions / Understanding)
5. Solutions Conversations
   (Problem Solving / Logic / Creativity / Innovation)
6. Commitment Conversations
   (Integrity / Values / Contracts / Agreements)
7. Discipline Conversations
   (Expectations / Criticism / Ramifications)
8. Empowerment Conversations
   (Enthusiasm / Inspiration / Motivation / Joy)
9. Appreciation Conversations
   (Compliments / Compensation / Reward)
10. Firing Conversations
    (Termination / Leaving / Ending / Retiring / Closure)

Hiring Conversations
(Meeting / Exploring / Interviewing / Auditioning)

- Hire slowly, spend some extra time. It will serve you in the long run.
- Reveal something of yourself, it helps others to open up.
- Know what you are looking for ahead of time. Explore ethics and values.
- Start by being objective, without bias. There is room for subjectivity later.
- Look for the most striking traits and examine inconsistent traits very closely.
- Observe carefully, scan from head to toe: hair, watch, fingernails, shoes.
- Compassion for others and satisfaction with life are key indicators.
- Focus on tone of voice, not just words and compare voice to body language.

Information Conversations
(Mentor / Learner / Questioning / Collaborating)

- Prepare for the conversation by focusing on the upcoming subject. Handle potential distractions.
- Get in touch with or create as much interest in the subject as you can.
- Work within your attention span. Take short breaks when necessary.
- Put strong emotion on what you most want to remember. Review the important points.
- Imagine a situation where you are remembering what you learned.

- Take notes or draw mind maps to help recall.

Decision Conversations
(Negotiating / Goal Setting / Reaching Conclusions)

- Choose the right people to help you decide. Run scenarios on possible outcomes.
- Make your goals specific, measurable, achievable, right, and timely.
- Avoid paralysis by analyses, wrong decisions might be better than no decisions.
- Know your ideal outcome(s) before beginning.
- Be sure that you have the relevant information.
- Remain open to hearing every side before deciding.
- Be willing to compromise without being compromised.

Empathy Conversations
(Sharing Feelings / Emotions / Understanding)

- Speak your truth without exaggeration.
- Listen with your heart more than your head. Let go of the need to be right.
- Be willing to listen without the need for solutions.
- Give feedback that you are both hearing and understanding.
- Put yourself as much as possible in the others shoes.
- Recall if you can when you were feeling the same way.
- Make eye contact and touch if appropriate.

Solutions Conversations
(Problem Solving / Logic / Creativity / Innovation)

- Brainstorm and let every idea be a good one.
- Use deductive logic and eliminate what won't work.

- Access the Alpha State to open up to the creativity of the HeartMind.
- Take alternative perceptions, see the problem from other points of view.
- Check your intuition to see what feels right. Look for more than one right answer.
- Run best case and worst case scenarios on each of the possible solutions.
- Curiosity–Research–Experimentation–Aha–Theory–Investigation–Verification–Engineering

Commitment Conversations
(Integrity / Values / Contracts / Agreements)
- Be certain that the timing is right for all participants.
- Express the importance of the upcoming discussion.
- Handle all distractions ahead of time to be fully present.
- Create an environment that is free of interruptions.
- Be sure that all language is clear, concise and fully understood.
- Communicate your values and be consistent to them throughout.
- Be certain that your head and heart are in agreement.

Discipline Conversations
(Expectations / Criticism / Ramifications)
- Begin and end with appreciation and put the criticism in between.
- Be certain that all parties are very clear on all of the expectations.
- Express your optimism that things can be worked out.
- Describe whatever behavior or attitude that isn't working.
- Express the way that you feel about it.
- Specify the attitude or behavior change that you desire.
- Share first the positive consequence that changing will bring.

- If the behavior persists then describe the negative consequences that not changing will bring.

Empowerment Conversations
(Enthusiasm / Inspiration / Motivation / Joy)

- Express the way that you feel about the person's potential.
- Let them know that you are aware of their accomplishments.
- Use enthusiasm and passion in your voice and mannerisms.
- Help them develop greater interest in achieving the desired outcome.
- Give them a sense of ownership in that outcome.
- Make them feel that they are an essential part of the team.

Appreciation Conversations
(Compliments / Compensation / Reward)

- Create an environment that is free of distraction or interruptions.
- Introduce this conversation and allow the listener to prepare.
- Help the listener to be comfortable and accepting of the praise.
- Be specific about exactly which attitudes or behaviors you appreciate.
- Share the importance of their contributions.
- Be sincere and not too effusive in the giving of compliments.
- Make sure to fit the reward to the person who is receiving it.
- Speak from the heart with emotion when praising.

Firing Conversations
(Termination / Leaving / Ending / Retiring / Closure)

- Let them know up front what is happening.

- Create an environment that is free of distraction or interruptions.
- Be specific about the reasons for this decision.
- Share the process by which this conclusion was reached.
- Be firm but come from a place of gentle power.
- Be complimentary and appreciative whenever possible.
- Ask for questions and responses to ensure clarity.
- End the conversation on a positive note.

Questions To Consider Before These Conversations

- With whom (or under what circumstances) am I likely to have one of these talks?
- Why are these talks important, and what benefits can I derive from doing it well?
- What are the possible consequences of doing it poorly?
- What expertise or strengths do I bring to these conversations?
- What are my weaknesses or areas of concern?
- What are my goals and what outcomes do I desire to create?
- What was one of the worst one of these talks I've ever had and why?
- What was one of the best of these talks I've ever had and why?
- Describe your ideal state of mind and heart that you'd like to feel during these conversations.
- Who do you know that is great at these conversations and why?

Selling Conversations

The sales force is in some ways the life-blood of any corporation. Discovering ways to motivate them effectively is a cornerstone to creating success. On one level, it is remarkably simple. In some ways, people are people, and we are all motivated by the same things. It seems as if we are all motivated by reward and punishment. Actually it is not the reward or the punishment that motivates us, it is the way it *feels* to be rewarded or punished. We are motivated to do things because it feels good if we do them, and it feels bad if we don't. We are unmotivated when there is no strong feeling either way. We are unmotivated when we are bored, apathetic, or indifferent. Motivation isn't strongly connected to the logic of the conscious mind. Motivation comes primarily from the subconscious mind; the mind of imagination, the mind of emotion.

We are motivated by a negative emotion called worry. For example, we might imagine what would happen if we fail to sell enough. We imagine what it would feel like to not being able to buy what we need. We imagine what it would feel like not to be able to pay the bills. The subconscious mind can not tell the difference between imagination and reality. Those bad feelings feel real, and we are motivated to do whatever we need to do, to avoid having them again. Being motivated by negative emotions such as doubt, fear, or worry does work to a certain extent. Unfortunately, there are some negative side effects. A certain amount of worry is natural. Once at least, we must take a look at the possibilities of what could go wrong. Take the worst case scenario out of the realm of the unknown, and see it for what it is. Then decide what to do if it happens.

What would you do if you did not make enough money in sales to be able to make it? How would you survive? Answering this question makes the possibility of failure much less frightening. To imagine failure once, and then make your best plan, is an effective way to use worry. It is when worry becomes a primary tool for self-motivation that we run into problems. Excessive worry lowers our self esteem, and while it may push us away from failure, it also holds us back from success. All in all, being motivated by positive emotions such as happiness, confidence, and satisfaction works better. It feels better when we imagine reward, than it does if we imagine punishment, and there are some wonderful side effects. Our self esteem increases, success at sales becomes habitual, and we begin to improve in many other areas of our lives as well. Greatness at any endeavor spills over into every endeavor.

We are motivated by positive emotions when we dream, when we fantasize, when we have a vision of what we want. The subconscious mind experiences the positive emotions that are generated by our imagination of our success. These emotions that are generated feel good, and the subconscious wants to repeat them. The feelings become the magnet that draws the subconscious mind into repeating the experience.

We are all inherently motivated by what feels good. Your best results come when you help your sales force individually determine what would feel best to them. Help them determine their goals, as well as what feelings they will feel once they achieve them.

Here are some exercises to help motivate sales.

- What is your goal (sales or income) for the next 12 months? The next quarter? The next thirty days? Imagine you have already achieved it.

- What is the most (this side of impossible) you can imagine making?

- What comes to mind when you imagine yourself tremendously successful?

- What does success look like? What picture do you see?
  Example: Sitting in a limousine looking at bank books and stock certificates worth hundreds of thousands of dollars.

- What does success sound like? What words or sounds do you hear?
  Example: My accountant telling me that I am financially independent and that I am secure for the rest of my life.

- What does success feel like? What emotions are you feeling? What physical sensations are you experiencing? What intuitions do you have?
  Example: I feel powerful and confident. I feel a sense of expansion in my upper torso. I have a big smile on my face and a strong feeling in my heart that things are only going to keep getting better and better.

When it comes to educating your sales force, you must be able to communicate with them in their language, and you must be sure that the right stuff will come out, by putting the right stuff in. The employer is responsible to see to it that the sales force knows all about the products or services that are available. They must know every important detail about manufacture or operation. They must be prepared to answer any logical question that a customer might have. In addition, the sales force must have an up to date understanding of who the customers are and what the current condition of the marketplace is. But most important of all, the members of the sales force must understand their own strengths and weaknesses. What motivates them and what brings up their doubt and fear. What triggers in them enthusiasm and what creates boredom, apathy, or indifference. They must know who they are, and how they best sell.

Exercises to help you better understand your relationship to sales and selling.

- Remember one of your earliest memories of watching someone buying something from a salesperson. What do you remember about the dialogue? Describe the buyer. What do you imagine that they were feeling? Describe the seller. What do you imagine that they were feeling? What early lesson might you have learned about sales from this experience?

- As you were growing up, what do you remember your family saying about salespeople?

- What was the first major purchase you ever made? What do you remember about the seller? How did you decide when and where to buy it? How did you feel when you did?

- What was the most important purchase that you ever made? What do you remember about the seller? How did you decide when and where to buy it? How did you feel when you did?

- What was the first thing you remember selling? What thoughts and feelings went through you?

- Who is the greatest salesperson that you've seen? What makes the greatest salespeople great?
- What are your greatest assets as a salesperson? What are your greatest liabilities?
- What are your greatest blocks and resistances to changing?
- What has motivated you the most in the past?
- What is motivating you the most right now?
- What would you imagine could motivate you the most in the future?
- What else would you say about your sales skills?

Peak Performance

A powerful application of the state of Focused Passion is mental and emotional rehearsal. Rehearsing it in your mind/spirit/heart. I think the best line I ever heard on the subject I believe came from the man I think is the greatest golfer of all time.

Jack Nicklaus was asked about the secret to his incredible success, and he said, "I never hit a shot, not even in practice, without having a very sharp, in-focus picture of it in my head. First I see the ball where I want it to finish, nice and white and sitting up high on the bright green grass. Then the scene quickly changes, and I see the ball going there: its path, trajectory, and shape, even its behavior on landing. Then there is a sort of fade-out, and the next scene shows me making the kind of swing that will turn the previous images into reality."

You actually play the shot on auto-pilot, without thought just as you have rehearsed it. Your mind/spirit/heart knows just how to do it exactly right. You have imagined everything about this success. What it would look like, sound like, and most of all what it would feel like. Now do it. Someone asked Yogi Berra what he thought of when he hit the baseball, and Yogi so eloquently replied, "How can anybody think and hit at the same time?"

If you want to use Alpha to become more prosperous (and why not, you deserve it, and humanity needs your philanthropy) you must first understand that prosperity is a consciousness, it is not about your income. You can be prosperous with a small income and fail to be prosperous with a giant one. It's not what comes in that counts. It's how much stays and grows.

The proof is if you take a person with "poverty consciousness," you know, the ones that are always broke, always in debt, always late with their bills. Take a person like this and give them a lot of money. What happens is that they blow it all and find themselves deeper in debt than they were when they started. On the other hand, if you take a person with "prosperity consciousness" and strip them of every penny, what happens is, they figure out a way to get it all back again. It's clearly a consciousness. The vast majority of people have neither, most people have "break even consciousness."

To create "prosperity consciousness" you close your eyes . . . take a deep breath . . . and imagine yourself in your peaceful place. Imagine you are more prosperous. Imagine that you've got a lot of discretionary income to give to causes that you believe in. Imagine that the future is secure, and the kids educations are paid for. Imagine yourself driving that new car or relaxing in that beautiful vacation home or whatever best symbolizes prosperity. Make it seem as real as you can by evoking as much passion as possible.

This is the key. Imagine what you want, as if you have already got it, imagine it over and over again, and by far most important— IMAGINE DOING IT WITH GREAT PASSION!!

Most students suffer from Test Taking Anxiety at least some of the time. Some suffer every time. A lot of this performance anxiety is a direct response to the natural and normal fear of the unknown. Mental rehearsal (imagining in your mind/spirit/heart taking this test) is very important in creating familiarity and overcoming this fear.

If you're going into the Alpha Brainwave State to prepare yourself to do great on a test, you close your eyes and go to your peaceful place (as the doorway into Alpha) and then imagine yourself waking up in the morning thinking, "Today is my test, and I am ready."

Imagine yourself getting up, going to school, and sitting down at your desk. Imagine your teacher passing out the test, and the all of a sudden you are in a different place in the classroom, invisible, watching yourself taking the test.

You are too far away to see what questions the teacher is asking, and too far away to see what answers you are writing, but what you can see, from your invisible vantage point, what you can see, is the smile on your face and the gleam in your eye, and the way the pen is just moving so confidently down the page. You know what you look like when you are doing great, and that is exactly what you look like. Imagine finishing the test, putting down your pen and watch yourself nodding and smiling as you check to see that all your answers are correct. The bell rings and you walk out the door, and then you imagine that it is instantly the next class day. You imagine walking back into the classroom, imagine the teacher passing out the corrected exams, imagine seeing a big red **A** on top of yours, and you get very, very, excited.

Reading and Learning

One of my favorite examples of changing a habit involves one of my greatest passions which is reading. The key is changing your reading habit from reading the way you talk to reading the way you think. The problem with traditional speed reading programs is that they all have a fatal flaw. They ask you to do two things at the same time. In traditional speed reading programs they instruct you in such a way that part of your mind is supposed to be paying attention to how you are reading, and part of your mind is supposed to be paying attention to what you are reading. And, if you're doing those two things at the same time, you are in Beta, the state of divided attention. Being in Beta means that the filter closes down between minds and the information doesn't get as strongly imprinted in memory, so we have poor comprehension, and retention of the information.

What I'd like to do, is introduce you to the subject of accelerated reading from the point of view of how we learn to read in the first place, and then I'll show you where you can go. You learned something by five years old that was perhaps the most challenging learning task that you've ever faced.

Something that was more difficult than Law School, more complicated than Medical School. You learned something by five that was most likely the single most difficult learning task you will ever face, and it was called The Alphabet. Some think, "what are you talking about, The Alphabet, that's as easy as ABC." Others realize that it is incredibly complex learning task. Let me show you the process of how you learned the alphabet. The first thing is learning the noises of the letters. Most people learned it the same way, by singing, "The Alphabet Song."

"ABCD EFG HIJK LMNO P," at first I thought "LMNO" was one letter.

> "When I tried speed reading," said BrainMind, "part of the time I was thinking about the new way my eyes were supposed to move, and I lost comprehension, and part of the time I forgot to move my eyes in that new way because I got caught up in comprehending the material. It was confusing, and I didn't enjoy it because most of the time I wasn't giving my all to either one."
>
> "The key," said HeartMind, "is to teach me how and then you can focus on what. Once I am programmed to read at great speed, you are out of the reading rut. I will focus on the process of reading, and you, on what it means. This makes reading seem less like talking, and more like dreaming dreams."

We first learned the sounds of the letters through the song. But then it starts to get complicated, when they show us A and they say to us: that's pronounced "aye." And we think, OK, if you say so, great. But realize, they could have shown us one of these Œ and they could have said that's pronounced "aye," and we'd have gone, OK, if you say so, sure.

It's not like we knew what an "aye" looked like. It's not as if we would think, "well of course that A is an "aye," it looks just like an A-frame house. We simply didn't know. A is just a funny looking squiggle. Then they draw twenty six of these funny looking squiggles. And they named them all: aye, bee, cee, dee, etc. What if right now I drew a bunch of funny looking squiggles that you'd never seen before £ § ∑ ¥ π Ç Ω ∫ μ ¶ æ and I pronounce the first one "blar" and second one "ung" and third one "rvv," and the fourth one "zkk," how would you learn that? In order to learn it you'd have to make up a song: "bllar, ung, rvv, zkk" or something like that. In essence that is the first task in learning the alphabet. You have to memorize all these funny looking squiggles and all the names they are called. That, however, is not the hardest part in learning the alphabet.

After we memorize all the funny looking squiggles and their names, they show us one of these; **a**. Of course we run through our twenty six funny looking squiggles and we think, well it looks a little bit like an upside down **P**, but it's not an upside down **P**, and so we figure that it's not a letter! We know every one of the twenty six letters in the song, and that's not one of them. Then they tell us, well, actually that **a** is an "aye." And you think "What!? How can this **a** be an "aye"? You said this **A** is an "aye." The two "ayes" don't' look anything alike. This **A** is all straight lines, this **a** doesn't have any straight lines. And so they tell us this **A** is a big "aye" and this **a** is a little "aye . . ." Hold on! If this **A** is a big "aye" than this **A** is a little "aye."

Wait a minute, you mean to tell me that there are twenty six other funny looking squiggles that have the same name but look different? So they reply, no because you see little **c** looks just like big **C**. Little **b** looks about half like big **B**. Little **d** is half-backwards compared to big **D** and little **e** shows no resemblance whatsoever to big **E**. What's the rule here!?

I'm sorry, we don't have a rule, we just have twenty six other funny looking squiggles that may or may not resemble the original, except of course that they are pretty much interchangeable. Now we've got fifty two funny looking squiggles to memorize but we still haven't got to the hardest part. Then they show us one of these **A** things again, and they say "what's that?" And we say "aye." And they say, "good, what noise does it make?" And we say "aye," and they say well yeah, but it also happens to sound like "ahh," "aeh" or "auh."

The letter **C**, could be pronounced "cee" or "cah" or "chh." Somehow when you put the letter **P** together with the letter **H** it's not pronounced "p h," it's pronounced "f." And when you put these together T H R O U G H it is not pronounced "Ta ha ra oh yu ga ha" Somehow, that's pronounced "thru."

Take off the TH from the front and then it is pronounced "ruff." Take out the R from through and what is left, "though," is pronounced "Tho." By the time you end up memorizing all these letters, and all of the noises they make, with all of the strange combinations, and permutations, and variations, you've memorized tens of thousands of pieces of information, or independent variables.

Mastering the alphabet and learning to read involves learning more new information than anything you have ever faced. Not only did you learn it, you learned it so well that you've never forgotten any of it. Not for one moment. Never once in your whole life did you wonder what was that letter after B.

Never once in your whole life did you accidentally pronounce through as "Ta ha ra oh yu ga ha." You learned this information perfectly and permanently. It was one of the most difficult things you've ever learned, and you know it as well as your ABCs.

There were two reasons it seemed so easy. First, when you learned the alphabet you were in Alpha. You know how I know? Because five year olds live in Alpha. They are almost always in Alpha. Second, when you learned the alphabet, taught to you by your parents or perhaps a teacher, they taught it to you, thinking/feeling, "Of course you're going to learn the alphabet, everybody learns the alphabet." It never occurred to them that you wouldn't learn it, and, therefore, it never occurred to you.

After the alphabet comes the next step, where they take a few of those letters and they put them together, to make a word. CAT was my first spelling word, I don't know why, since we had a DOG, but nonetheless, it was my Mom's decision and she decided that CAT would be my first word.

She asked me what it spelled, and of course I knew what it spelled (I knew my alphabet). I told her, "It spells C - - A - - T." And she said, "yeah, but what does it spell." I said, "I told you, it spells C -- A -- T." And then she said that phrase that you heard thousands of times growing up. You remember the phrase? It goes like this, "Sound it out!"

So we pronounce the noises that each of the letters make, c a t , c a t . . . CAT! Oh yeah, that feline four legged creature that goes Meow, I know what that is.

But at five years old you could have looked at the letters C A T and had no idea what it was until you sounded it out. You had to make the noise because the picture the letters made was meaningless. You hadn't seen that before.

So, in order to read there are four things that you have to do:
1. First you see the word.
2. Then you hear the word.
3. Then you recognize the word.
4. Then you connect the word to it's meaning.

SEE, HEAR, RECOGNIZE, CONNECT

That's how you learned to read, and that's how you still read today. To this day, nothing has changed. You look at the word, you sound it out, you hear it in your head, you recognize that you know what that means, and then you move to the next word.

At twelve years old I began developing my own accelerated reading program. I loved reading fast, but the traditional speed-reading classes that I'd had, took all of the joy out of reading.

So what happened was, I had a dream. A powerful dream, and in my dream there were these two voices competing for attention. There was this one voice telling me, "You've got to read more. There's so much knowledge out there. You've got to learn more from all the brilliant men and women that have ever lived. Read more. Read more. Read more.

However this other voice was saying, "You've got to do Alpha more. You've got to learn from yourself. Know thyself. You're your own greatest teacher. Go inside and learn from yourself. Do More Alpha, More Alpha, More Alpha.

So one voice said, "Read More," the other voice said, "Alpha More," back and forth, "Read More, Alpha More, Read More, Alpha More." Then this extremely loud, deep, voice that came right from the core center of my being said, "Why don't you do them both at the same time?" And I woke up and I thought, "What a great idea." So I knew the basic idea of speed reading, learning to read more than one word at a time. We began by reading individual letters, we moved to reading groups of letters or syllables, and then to reading groups of syllables or words. The next step is reading groups of words. Reading whole concepts or ideas. When you read the phrase "in the house," First you read "in," you see the word "in," you say it to yourself, you recognize what means, the opposite of out, and then you move to the next word. You look at the word "the" and you ask yourself what does "the" mean, and of course you don't know. I never knew anybody who knew what the word "the" meant. It's one of the most common words in the English language, and we have no idea what it means. My best guess is that it means "proceed to the next word." Then we see the word "house" and most people first see the image of the outside of a house, before they correlate the data and recognize, oh, "in the house," and what that whole concept means. It takes three looks to recognize "in the house."

Yet whenever you read one single long word (such as the word "Psychologist") one look and you can instantly recognize what that is. It takes three times as long to read "in the house" as it does to read the single word "psychologist" though they are both the same size. If you know a word, regardless of it's size, you can instantly recognize it and then move on to the next word.

The idea is training the mind/spirit/heart to read phrases such as "in the house" all at once, moving out of reading the way you talk, and into reading the way you think. No matter how fast you talk you can't say more than one word at a time, but you can think many. So, no matter how fast you read, you'll still hear words in your mind, but you'll hear then as thoughts instead of as self talk. Thinking happens at a speed much greater than talking does. Thinking doesn't seem faster, but it certainly is. The only thing you notice as you develop these accelerated reading techniques is that you're turning pages quicker, and finishing books sooner. Exceptional readers are the ones who go beyond, and see several words, even several sentences in one fixation.

The ability to move beyond the old "one word at a time" technique is the key to mastering the art of accelerated reading. The movement pattern of the eyes, a very powerful habit unchanged in most since adolescence, is the single most basic sub-habit of reading. It is, therefore, very closely related to all the other sub-habits. By changing that one most basic reading sub-habit, we create a "blank slate" effect. The other sub-habits such as comfort, posture, breathing, concentration, retention, level of interest and attention span are no longer automatic as when they were connected to and triggered by the "one word at a time" eye movement technique.

By learning to read in a *new way* (more than one word at a time) we can discard any of the old sub-habits that no longer serve us and integrate anything we choose into the new reading habit.

Just knowing that we can take a habit as intensely ingrained as reading one word at a time, and, through the use of Alpha programming, change it permanently can be a very powerful tool. The first new step in accelerated reading is to break the habit of focusing on each word individually. The key is learning a new habit of focusing on several words at the same time. The first step is the "tri-focus" technique. This means to focus three times per line. To focus on a third of a line at a time.

First Focus Left, Then The Center, Then To The Right.

I could tell people to read with this tri-focus technique, and they could, but when you divide your attention between how you are reading (the new way of moving your eyes in the tri-focus), and understanding what you are reading (comprehending the information) it makes reading hard work, and takes all of the joy out of pleasure reading. This is the fatal flaw in traditional speed reading programs.

Reading in a state of divided attention (the Beta State) is ineffective. So instead of consciously trying to tri-focus, what we will do is program the mind/spirit/heart to tri-focus automatically. We will utilize Alpha to reprogram the movement of the eyes. Doing this allows the new eye movement (tri-focus) to happen automatically, leaving the mind free to pay total attention to comprehending the material.

The first step is to go into Alpha (eyes closed, deep breath, peaceful place), focus and relax. In the Alpha Brainwave State we begin the process of recreating our reading by imagining the vehicle that we will use to create change, and that vehicle is a "Magic Book." The Magic Book is the key to changing the reading habit.

Begin by creating the cover of the book in your mind. Make this cover as magical as possible. It could be solid gold, jewel encrusted, ancient hand tooled leather, or something that E.T. brought on his last visit. It could smell like roses, make beautiful music when you touch it, and it could even float in the air. This is a *magical book* and the laws of reality need not apply.

The secret to empowering this Magic Book is extremely simple. Just how much can you L O V E this book? Now what I've done with my Magic Book, is I've taken some of my favorite memories and favorite fantasies, and things that I LOVE the most in the whole world, and I've put these things in my Magic Book. It could be anything, anything at all. No law of the physical universe has anything to do with this book. It could look like solid gold and yet it could float, and smell like roses, and it could feel like raw silk. I can be anything, real or imaginary, that you choose. But remember, the key is just how much can you L O V E this book.

This is what I did to L O V E mine. I remembered times from my life that I felt the most love ever. One time, when I was 5 years old, and walking down the sidewalk with my Mom, I looked in this big plate glass window, and there in the Pet Shop was the cutest little puppy dog you've ever seen. I turned to my Mom and I said, "Mommy, PLEASE can I have this puppy dog?" And she said yes. She'd sort of been thinking about getting me a dog and so we walked into this Pet Shop and they sold me that doggy in the window, and I walked out carrying that puppy, and she was licking my face, and I L O V E D that puppy, and I took that feeling of LOVE, and I put it in my Magic Book, so I L O V E my Book. But that's not enough.

I wanted to love this book as much or more than I've ever loved anything, so I left reality and ventured into fantasy. So every time I

51

touch my Magic Book, every hungry baby in the world gets fed, and I L O V E that, so of course I L O V E My Magic Book.

As we open up this Magic Book, we notice is that this book has no words in it.

Tri-Focus Exercise

--------*--------   --------*--------   --------*--------

--------*--------   --------*--------   --------*--------

--------*--------   --------*--------   --------*--------

--------*--------   --------*--------   --------*--------

--------*--------   --------*--------   --------*--------

--------*--------   --------*--------   --------*--------

We imagine the page filled not with words but instead with the tri-focus exercise. No words! This Magic Book isn't about **what** to read, it's about **how** to read. To practice this tri-focus exercise, just focus your eyes three times per each line.

Focus left,	then center,	then right.
Focus left,	then center,	then right.
Focus left,	then center,	then right.
Focus left,	then center,	then right.

The imaginary book must be read with the tri-focus exercise at every opportunity. After X number of repetitions, it becomes a habit. If you bring great passion or emotional amplitude to the practice, you can lower the number of repetitions that are required. Time means very little, **times** (repetitions) means a lot. Once the habit (automatic behavior) is established, it is no longer necessary to practice with the imaginary book tri-focus exercise because the habit reinforces itself.

Create the tri-focus in Alpha and allow it to spill over automatically into regular reading. Intentionally tri-focus only in your Magic Book. Whenever you are reading anything for real, allow your eyes to do whatever they do all by themselves. It is very important to remember to intentionally tri-focus only in your Magic Book.

Once the tri-focus begins to happen automatically, it is time to program the other preferred sub-habits associated with reading. Focused concentration, comfortable posture, holding the book at eye level, and rhythmic breathing are a few of the basics. Along with enhanced attention span, efficient page turning, and reading with eyes opened wide.

Programming a powerful positive belief "I will understand and recall everything I need from everything I read" is also a must. Program all this by going into the Alpha Brainwave State and imagining reading with these sub-habits already in place. Feel your intense connection and get a sense of how quickly the pages are turned.

By investing a little bit of time now (lots of 20 second Alpha exercises) to read three to five times faster, you will save yourself months, even years over the course of the rest of your life. I knew the basics of accelerated reading techniques, and I knew the basics of Alpha Programming. Going to my peaceful place, and imagining what I truly want, over and over, as if I already have it, and do it with GREAT PASSION! So I went to Alpha through my peaceful place, and I asked myself how to program my mind/spirit/heart to read faster and read better. To read more than one word at a time. This is exactly what I imagined.

Alpha Exercise

I saw myself in my Peaceful Place, my calm, serene, and tranquil space
I slowed my pace, I stopped the chase, as a great big smile came upon my face
And then from my quiet place of peace, I saw ahead a trail,
That winds into the forest, over hill and dale.
A trail that leads me to learning. To a special spot that awaits.
Up ahead, round the bend is my Learning Laboratory, behind two golden gates.
I walked up to those gates of gold, reached out my hands and grabbed a hold,
I opened those gates and I stepped inside, to where accelerated learning resides,
Where I write my story in my Learning Laboratory.
I felt I was getting smarter, with every single breath I'd take.
Getting ready for the changes that I was about to make.
As I looked into my Lab, across the room over there,
What I saw was what looked like a most comfortable chair.
So I went and sat myself down over there.
Next to the chair on the floor was a safe, the heavy metal kind,
With a combination dial and I checked it out to find,
That the first three numbers that came to my mind would open the safe.
So with those three numbers from my mind, I opened the safe.
I opened it up, and took a look, what I found inside was my Magic Book.
Not solid gold, nor encrusted with jewels, not ancient leather made of ancient tools.
My cover was of a substance that I'd never before seen,
I let my imagination create the vivid dream.
A liquid rainbow cover, my Magic Book possessed,
And every time I touched it, I knew that I was blessed.
For every hungry person everywhere, my Magic Book would feed
Every time I touched it, I helped billions who were in need
That's what it took to help me LOVE MY BOOK
Yes, that's what it took to help me LOVE MY BOOK
I took a look at my Magic Book, I opened it up inside,

As I knew I would, what I then saw, was the tri-focus exercise.
Three lines where in a book there would have been words before
But this Magic Book has three lines, no less, and no more.
So left, center, right, I moved my eyes, doing the tri-focus exercise.
Basking in the passion that I would feel, pretending my Magic Book was real.
Again and again I moved my eyes. Doing the tri-focus exercise.
Moving my eyes with great emotion. Doing the tri-focus with great devotion.
Feeling the PASSION I moved my eyes, repeating the tri-focus exercise.
Then I imagined that I was able to read, with great comprehension at very fast speed.
With magnificent retention of everything I'd read,
And brilliant recollection of anything I'd need,
I imagined it true, that my reading skills grew,
Great reading was something I could already do.
The tri-focus exercise I did adore.
I woke up, went back, and did it several times more.

In Alpha, program with passion, "every time I read I read in the tri-focus." Then again with even more passion, "every time I read I read in the tri-focus." When I read with the tri-focus my concentration is total and complete. Every time I read I read in the tri-focus."

Whenever you read always hold the page up at eye level, and not down on your desk or in your lap. This is very important because when you hold the book down in your lap or flat on a desk, and you look down at the top of the page, your eyelids are half shut. What happens as you read down the page is that your eyelids are slowly closing. When you finally reach the bottom of the page, your eyelids are 90% shut. You almost always fall asleep at the bottom of a page. Rarely do you fall asleep at the top of the page. If you have enough energy to turn the page and look up to the top of the next page, then you're awake. You virtually always fall asleep at the bottom of the page.

People fall asleep not necessarily because they're bored, but because of the physiology involved in reading like this. Your head nods, breathing gets shallow. When your brain gets short of oxygen, you yawn. What happens when you yawn? You think/feel either bored or tired. Always read with the plane of the page parallel to the plane of your face, never perpendicular. When you hold the page parallel to the plane of your face, all the words are pretty much equally distant from your eyes But when you hold the page perpendicular like on a desk, the words on top of the page are three times as far away from your eyes as the words on the bottom of the page are.

Reading this way means that you are asking your eyes to work harder, because, in addition to moving left and right and down the page, you are asking your eyes to adjust frequently in yet another way, they have to telescope in, telescope in, telescope in, adjusting for distance with every new line. This telescoping muscle of the eye is the very weakest. We are not used to looking far, then closer, then closer, then closer. That muscle's the weakest of the eye muscles. So always hold the plane of the face parallel to the plane of the page when you read.

One of the keys to comprehension, when you are reading, is interest. Interest is a fascinating concept, but interest has little to do with what you're doing. Interest comes from the past or the future. You are interested in something now because something happened in the past leading you to believe that learning this now is going to feel good. Or you're interested in something now because you think by doing this now, something that feels good is going to happen in the future. Interest has little to do with what you're doing. It comes from memory or fantasy.

Quite often we are not conscious of these memories or fantasies, they are below our level of conscious awareness. Real or imaginary things that feel good create the phenomena called interest. One time, to create passionate interest in a physics class I feared would be boring, I imagined I was walking out of my class carrying my physics book in my hand and walking across campus to my bank. I walked in carrying my physics book in one hand and my check book in the other, and as I got in line at the bank, I noticed that standing in front of me in line, the next person in line, was the woman of my dreams. There she was, Venus in blue jeans, Aphrodite in a halter top. Everything, everything, everything I'd ever dreamed of in a woman was standing right in front of me. Even from the back I knew, she was the one for me. I'm imagining that I'm staring at her, and she turned around and she looked at me, and her eyes met my eyes and my eyes met her eyes and cupid's arrows were shot into both of us and there were flowers and hearts and angels and rainbows and it was love, it was love at first sight, it was the most incredible love, it was the most wonderful love. We stared at each other, wondering where we had been all of each other's lives and then all of a sudden I noticed she started looking down at my physics book, and so for the first time I looked down and I noticed she was carrying a copy of that same physics book!! What an amazing coincidence!!

She looked at my physics book I looked at her physics book, our eyes met once again and she said to me, "Oh you're taking physics, I'm having oh so much trouble with that."

I said, "Well fair maiden allow me to be of assistance."

So we went over to this coffee shop across the street from the campus, and she said, "Do you really understand physics?"

And I said, "Well of course I do."

At that moment, I opened my eyes for real, I picked up my physics book for real, and opened it up and I read the first paragraph, for real. I closed the physics book, closed my eyes, imagined my peaceful place and then, the restaurant, and there she was again, and she said, "What did it say?"

And I told her what it said and she said, "Oh you're so smart" and she started holding my hand as we started studying together. We studied together for our first physics exam and we both got As and came back together and congratulated each other and we started studying together all semester long. About half way through the semester I had a really brilliant idea and I decided to make her a better physics student than I was. Now all of a sudden she's picking up on this stuff faster than I am and she's saying, "What's the matter, don't you get it?"

I'd say, "Well give me a minute, my male ego's being challenged." This exercise with my Physics Girl changed my academic life dramatically. To this day I truly love physics.

Six Part Study Skills System

1. **Scan**: Look over the material before you read it. Warm up the mind on the subject matter before you begin to study.

2. **Psyche up**: Get yourself interested in the material that you are about to study. Imagine why it actually is important to you or else make up a reason that motivates you to pay attention.

3. **Read**: Read with total focused concentration in alpha using the tri-focus technique for the duration of your attention span.

4. **Process with confidence**: In eyes closed Alpha, imagine that you are fully confident that you know the information and will be able to recall it anytime, especially under pressure.

5. **Review**: Go back over what you just read, very quickly over what you realized that you already knew. Go very quickly over what you totally understood. Go very quickly over what you don't need to know, and stop and study only what is left. Review what you know, study only what you didn't get the first time through.

6. **Rehearse**: Imagine watching yourself taking a test. Watch the smile on your face as you successfully answer questions. See yourself checking your answers knowing you got them right. Imagine handing in and received back the corrected test. Imagine the A or 100% and finish by congratulating yourself on a great performance.

Perhaps the single most dangerous thing our school system does, is force children to take classes they're not interested in. When you attempt to learn something you're not interested in you usually don't learn it very well and, therefore, you feel less intelligent. Your self esteem goes down, and so does your ability to heal. We don't need to force children to take classes they're not interested in. We already have existing today, the technology to entice them to.

Just hire creative people like those who come up with ideas like Teenage Mutant Ninja Turtles to make commercials for English classes. Kids will be saying, "please, please, let me take English."

A key to taking in information is paying attention. We know several things already about paying attention. We know that Alpha is the state of attention, so before you read anything, close your eyes and go to your peaceful place first. You always focus your attention on your peaceful place so now you have a focused attention state to shift over to the material you're about to read.

Now, instead of hoping the material will bring you into a focused concentration state, you focus your concentration first on your peaceful place and then shift over to the material you are learning. Another thing about paying attention is that it is much easier to pay attention to something when you have some kind of idea what you're going to pay attention to before you pay attention to it. Its much easier to move into the process of learning, when the mind/spirit/heart is warmed up. So step one, you scan the material. This is not reading, or even skimming. You take a look at what you're about to read, just looking at a few words on each page, the words that pop out at you, just thinking about what subject this is, before you read it.

The reason for this is that one of the most basic of all human experiences is the fear of the unknown. When you take a book that you haven't read before, and you look at what you're about to read your eye is a camera it actually takes a picture. (We all have a photographic memory, though some of us develop the film better than others, we all take pictures.) Go back and read the material and it seems no longer unknown. There is an instant recollection, an immediate affinity for what feels familiar. Always look over the material you wish to study before you read it.

If you're already interested in what you're about to read then get in touch with that interest and amplify it. If you're not interested in what you're about to learn, then create interest in it. When you read, you read for the duration of your attention span. It's fine that we have a limited attention span because it doesn't really matter. Five minutes are as good as twenty minutes because regardless of the duration of your attention span you have an incredibly rapid recovery rate. You can pay attention to something for five minutes, then take ten seconds off (Imagine your peaceful place induction) and you're ready to go again for five more minutes. Pay attention for five more minutes, take ten seconds off, and you're ready for five more.

It doesn't matter how long your attention span is. Because you have an incredibly rapid recovery rate. When you study, distractions and interruptions can be GOOD. If I'm studying and all of a sudden I hear this truck go by, that's good, because my attention had begun to fade enough so that the truck captured it. I didn't hear the previous trucks go by. I only heard that truck because I wasn't giving my full attention to what I was reading any more. When you get interrupted, or distracted, that gives you an opportunity to go to Alpha and get a brand new attention span.

If you are reading and you have this internal distraction, this thought that says, "You need to do your laundry!" What you need to do then (to keep the distraction from reoccurring) is to make a decision. You need to decide when you are going to do laundry (Thursday 4 PM) or decide when to decide when to do your laundry (after this chapter).

It is important to process the information effectively. One of the most interesting things about the process of memory is that when information comes in there is short term memory and long term memory. Short term memory is very temporary, lasts for just a few moments. Long term memory is anything that lasts more than those few moments and what happens with long term memory it goes into permanent memory storage.

There is no middle term memory. If it makes it into long term its there forever. Memory is perfect, the ability to recall is what breaks down. The various places information goes in the memory bank, has nothing to do with the information itself at all. If you imagine your memory bank being like a series of filing cabinet drawers with the easy to remember stuff in the front and the hard to remember stuff in the back, where information goes in that memory bank has nothing to do with the information. What it has to do with entirely is something I call the emotional rider.

The emotion you feel about the information is what determines where in the memory bank it goes. You remember what you love, you remember what you hate, and you remember what scares you, you re-member what excites you, what you don't remember is what you didn't care about, what bored you, what you were apathetic about. The more emotion, the easier anything is to remember, and the less emotion, the harder everything is to remember.

The key to processing information is doing it with emotion. This works with real emotion or pretend emotion because the subconscious mind doesn't know the difference between imagination and reality. As I finish reading, I stop for a moment and I say to myself, with great passion "GOT IT." I put that emotion of intense confidence onto the information I just learned and then it files into my memory bank along with everything else I feel that confident about.

It goes right next to, how to tell time, how to tie my shoes, what my brother's name is. Process information, put an emotion on it, before it goes into your memory bank.

The real key to learning technical material is effectively reviewing what you've learned. When you're reading technical material go through it once and let yourself miss stuff, its okay because you know you're going to go back. Get the basic idea, the first time through. Let yourself miss stuff, don't reread, continue to read onward, feeling it's okay to come back and get it next time through. When you go back you go very fast over the material that when you realized you already knew that. You go very fast over the material that you realized def-initely understood. You go very fast over the material that you realized doesn't matter, and you stop, and you carefully study what you still need to learn. "Great students only study what they don't know, they don't study what they know."

Read it once through for the purpose of getting most of it and then go back really quickly and only stop and pick out the pieces you missed the first time. If you like to underline or overline or take notes on what you are studying, this is where you do it.

You need not underline the first time you read something. The purpose of underlining is to prioritize, to determine what's more important than what. How are you going to do that effectively, when you don't know what you've got to work with yet. Finally, you practice remembering. This is an example of Mental Rehearsal in the Alpha State to create Peak Performance.

If you were a student and you had a history test on Friday, you would start your practicing a week before. You would close your eyes, take a deep breath, and go to your Peaceful Place. Next you would imagine yourself laying in your own bed waking up in the morning. Imagine your first thought is, "Today is Friday, today's my history test, and I'm ready." So you imagine getting up, feeling very confident, and going to school. As soon as you get to school you imagine that you sit down at your desk and the teacher passes out the exam, and as soon as you get the exam you imagine that an invisible part of you steps outside of yourself and is watching yourself from over there taking that exam. Imagine that you are a little to far away to see what questions are on that exam or what answers you are writing.

What you can see as you watch yourself, is your pen zooming along answering every question, and you can see that smile on your face, and that gleam in your eye. You know just what you look like when you are doing great, and that's what you look like. Imagine finishing with lots of time left, put down the pen, pick up the answer sheet, checking your answers, nodding smiling, saying, yes, yes, yes, yes. You hand in the exam, the bell rings and you walk out of the room. As soon as you get out of the room you imagine that it's the next class day, you walk back into your class, the teacher passes the corrected exam back with a big red A on top and you say ALL RIGHT!! Imagine this about fifteen times a day for a week before the exam. When you walk into that exam on Friday, for real, your subconscious mind is going to think/feel, "Oh this exam again—I've taken this exam a hundred times, I always get an A on this exam.

"I've got a habit of getting an A on this exam." What happens is, that all the answers that are in your mind will come out. Now of course this only works if you study, but if the information is in there it knows how to come out. This virtually eliminates the tip of the tongue syndrome.

"So," said BrainMind, "I go to Alpha through my peaceful place, and I scan the material to warm up my mind. Then I warm up my heart by getting in touch with or creating interest. Next I read and take in the information only for the duration of my attention span. I stop and then I put a strong emotion on what I just read. I quickly review the material and then last, I rehearse remembering what's important."

"Right," said HeartMind, "We go to Alpha to begin, I bring the passion, and you focus in. We scan what we're reading to warm up the mind. It gives me a head start, I know what I'll find. Then I add the passion, the interest to read, and then you take it in at a really fast speed. Then I'll put strong emotion on what we just read, to process it right in our heart and our head. Then you review quickly, decide what we will need, go over the rest at incredible speed. Last we rehearse what we need to recall, pretending inside we remember it all. These six steps will always allow us to learn. We now have a system to which we can turn."

Gaining Confidence

"What can you tell me," said BrainMind, "about becoming more confident?"

HeartMind replied, "Go inside and do explore, what feels good and what feels sore. What feels strong and what feels weak, what you have and what you seek. What feels right inside of you, of all the things you say and do, and what is there that you must change, that calls for you to rearrange. Develop confidence, more each day, release what's wrong in a gentle way. Focus your mind on what feels the best, gaining confidence to heal the rest. No need now to fight your way up the stream,

> just follow the wave of self esteem. With confidence dreams come true, as all love flows through your own love for you."

Sharon, single and in her late twenties, had been working for several years as a dispatcher for a local trucking company. She would tell the drivers where to pick up their loads and give them the directions to the deliveries. The job was pretty routine, and not very challenging. Through the grapevine she learned that the woman who was the executive assistant to the president of the company was about to retire. Sharon very much wanted that job, and she knew she could learn how to do it. The problem was that she didn't have enough confidence to ask the president of the company for the opportunity. "I think that I can do it" Sharon thought. "It's just that every time I even consider mentioning it to anyone, my stomach starts churning and my knees turn to jelly. My mouth gets dry and my palms get sweaty. I get really scared. I'm afraid people will think that I can't do it. I'm afraid that if I do ask and they say no, it will jeopardize my current job. I'm even a little afraid that maybe I can't do it, that I'm not as capable as I think I am." Sharon knew she needed some assistance. She went looking for something that could help her build up her confidence and get over her fear.

She was looking for tools or techniques that could teach her how to build her courage and confidence. Then she learned about the power of Focused Passion. First she closed her eyes, took a deep breath, and imagined her peaceful place. Sharon's peaceful place was a beach on the island of Maui. The sky was blue without even a cloud, the sun was bright and the water was warm. The sand was a brilliant white. She heard the sounds of the ocean waves crashing against the surf and felt the warmth of the white sand between her toes. Sharon took a few moments to pretend she was really there. She felt her body begin to relax and noticed her breathing was slowing down.

She began to feel calm and peaceful, alone on her beautiful beach. Next she began the process of sorting out her feelings. She asked herself, "How do I feel about going for the job?" And then was quiet as she paid attention to whatever thoughts and feelings came up for her. She imagined herself walking up to the boss, to say she was interested in the job. She observed herself getting more and more nervous the closer she got to him. When she got there she was too scared to mention it, and so she heard herself ask some silly question and after receiving the answer, saw herself walk back to her desk. The next thing she imagined was herself, a lot older, and a lot more tired, still sitting behind the same desk, a very uncomfortable thing to see.

She took a deep breath and slowly woke herself up and thought about what it all meant. She realized that the daydream pointed out her two basic fears. One fear was that she would look silly or stupid even asking for this job, much less trying to do it. The second fear was that if she didn't ask for this job she might just be doing this same old job forever. She realized that the second fear was much greater than the first one. The next step was to go back to Alpha and reprogram her mind. Sharon closed her eyes, took a deep slow breath, and went back to the same peaceful place. Once again she imagined herself at work, only this time she did so on purpose. In her imagination she saw herself get up from her desk and stand up straight and tall. She saw herself walk straight up to the president of the company, calm and confident, and tell him that she would be the perfect person for the job. In her mind, Sharon watched her boss look at her with newfound interest and respect as he told her he would consider her offer. She imagined walking back to her desk, walking very tall and feeling very, very proud of herself. Sharon imagined the president calling her into his office and telling her that she had the job. She felt tremendous joy and excitement at the new opportunity. She saw herself walking back to her old desk and cleaning out her things. She imagined moving into her new office and setting things up just the way she liked them. She focused on feeling just about as wonderful as a person possibly could feel.

Next Sharon imagined herself a little older, sitting in her office, the office of the executive assistant. She was looking at a copy of her annual employee evaluation in which the president had given her excellent marks in every area. Sharon sat for a moment and felt very, very proud of herself. She told herself, "I am a capable person who is worthy of this job. I am competent and confident and I deserve this opportunity." She took another deep breath and opened her eyes. Practicing this second Alpha technique eight or ten times a day for a week was what it took for Sharon to get up the courage to talk to her boss. Although it didn't go exactly as she imagined it (he was too busy to talk when she first approached) it eventually went just as she'd planned. She found a job that was much more interesting, and pays a lot better. She felt very proud of herself, and felt very courageous for taking the risk. Sharon used the Alpha State of Focused Passion to get in touch with the confidence she needed to overcome her doubts and fears.

In order to gain confidence, we must be willing to take risks. We must be able to see what we really want, and do it. Just as doubt leads to clarity, fear leads to confidence. Doubt gives us the opportunity to learn, fear gives us the opportunity to grow. Doubt and fear are like the yellow light on a traffic signal. They mean use your intuition to decide whether to go now, or wait a little while; until the direction is right, and the timing is right, and then, if it is right, to go. Either way, doubt and fear can lead to "go." Self confidence, self respect, self esteem, and self worth are all reflections of your self love. Which is a reflection of the way you have responded to the positive and negative suggestions that you have created and encountered.

Each time you receive a positive or negative suggestion, from yourself or somewhere else, you have the opportunity to influence your levels of self love. If you strongly agree with the positive suggestion, then your self-love goes up. If you strongly disagree with or discount the positive suggestion, then your self love goes down. It also works the other way too. If you strongly disagree with a negative suggestion, your self-love goes up; strongly agree with the negative suggestion, and your self-love goes down. Where you hold the level of your self love is especially significant when you realize that the only love that you can actually feel is your own self love.

All love flows through your own love for you!

When somebody loves you, it is not their love that you are feeling. Their love is inside of them. It is your own love for yourself that you are feeling, vibrating in harmony with the love they are feeling for you. To whatever extent you love yourself, that is how much love you can feel from another.

The more love you have for yourself, the more love you can evoke in someone else. Love is a reflection of the powerful life force as it flows through you. Increase your level of love and you increase your intelligence and your ability to heal. It's all the same force.

Relaxation Sensation

Close your eyes, take a deep breath, and imagine your peaceful place. Make this quiet peaceful place you've chosen seem as real as you can. Remember a time from your past when you felt especially good. Remember some accomplishment you achieved, or some special event that you attended. See (or pretend that you see) what surrounds you. Notice if there are any other people around, and if so, what expressions are on their faces. Listen (or pretend to listen) to the sounds that surround you. Imagine that you smell the smells. Notice in what part of your body you most feel the feelings that are associated with this place. Begin to exaggerate that feeling inside your body. Make it as powerful as your imagination will allow. Suggest that you will continue to feel these feelings. Whenever it feels comfortable for you, take a deep breath, open your eyes, come wide awake. Then get yourself up and with passion, take your next action step.

Getting Your Goals

Close your eyes, take a deep breath, and imagine your peaceful place. Make this quiet peaceful place you've chosen seem as real as you can. Allow yourself to imagine something that you've always wanted, as if it were coming true right this very moment. Let yourself imagine a goal, an accomplishment, or a dream. Notice the feelings that begin to emerge in your body as your imagination of this event becomes more and more vivid, more and more real. Intensify the emotions by focusing on where in your body you feel them. Hold onto the ever growing emotions inside your body. Feel them as they continue to build. Feel the conviction that the goal, dream, or accomplishment is coming true. Allow yourself to become more and more convinced. Whenever it feels comfortable for you, take a deep breath, open your eyes, come wide awake. Then get yourself up and with passion, take your next action step.

Listen To The Messenger

Close your eyes, take a deep breath, and imagine your peaceful place. Make this quiet peaceful place you've chosen seem as real as you can. Imagine that walking towards you, way off in the distance, is someone very special. This person is still too far away to recognize, but you have the strongest intuition that whoever it is, they are bringing you the best news that you've heard in a long long time. Allow that feeling to build inside you. Let the person come into view and notice whether you recognize them. Whether or not you do, get the feeling that you know them. When they get close enough to talk to you, listen to the wonderful news that they bring. Whenever it feels comfortable for you, take a deep breath, open your eyes, come wide awake. Then get yourself up and with passion, take your next action step.

Helping Out

Close your eyes, take a deep breath, and imagine your peaceful place. Make this quiet peaceful place you've chosen seem as real as you can. Imagine that joining you in your place of peace is someone who very much needs your help, the kind of help that you can give them. Imagine that they have a problem that you used to have, but have since solved. Sit down with them and share the solution you found for your problem. Watch how happy and relieved that this person becomes now that they know what to do about their problem. Imagine just how thankful they are that you took the time to help them out. Feel how it feels to have helped someone in need. Exaggerate that feeling and bask in the glow. Whenever it feels comfortable for you, take a deep breath, open your eyes, come wide awake. Then get yourself up and with passion, take your next action step.

Taking Compliments

Close your eyes, take a deep breath, and imagine your peaceful place. Make this quiet peaceful place you've chosen seem as real as you can. Imagine that one by one, all your closest friends from throughout your life come and join you in this place. Imagine friends from early childhood up through the friends that you have in your life today. Each one, in turn, walks right up to you, looks you in the eye and tells you something that they really like about you. Each one thanks you for being an important part of their life. After they finish, imagine sitting together and discussing how wonderful it is to be your friend. Thank them all for their love and support. Whenever it feels comfortable for you, take a deep breath, open your eyes, come wide awake. Then get yourself up and with passion, take your next action step.

Magic Mirror

Close your eyes, take a deep breath, and imagine your peaceful place. Make this quiet peaceful place you've chosen seem as real as you can. Imagine that you're standing in front of a full length mirror. It is a very beautiful mirror with a golden frame that surrounds it. The reflection that you see is of yourself, but with a few variations. The shoulders are up and back a little bit, your stance is tall and erect and yet relaxed. The expression on your face reflects a feeling of supreme confidence. You can tell from the sparkle in your eyes just how well everything is going. Get the feeling that the mirror is telling the real truth about you, the truth that you sometimes don't let yourself see. Feel the feeling of confidence growing inside of you as you stare into this Magic Mirror. Whenever it feels comfortable for you, take a deep breath, open your eyes, come wide awake. Then get yourself up and with passion, take your next action step.

Breaking Habits

"Habits are the key," said BrainMind. "The reason we are as good as we are, is the same reason that we are only as good as we are, our habits, our patterns, our operating system program."

HeartMind said, "Yes, habits are the key, program me right and I'll set you free. Some things we do, we consciously choose, we know it's deductive logic we use. Most things we do as we've done them before, simply habit, no less, no more, The way to break habits in most any case, is to find something to do to replace.

"Habits you had that serve you no more, a way that's better than the way before. Replace bad habits bothering you, with something a whole lot better to do, Program habits to help create doing things that are good in ways that are great."

Roy was overweight. His mother told him, his girlfriend told him, and now his doctor had told him in no uncertain terms. "Lose some weight, or you'll be asking for heart problems." That was the last thing Roy wanted to hear. As a young boy, he had lost his father to a heart attack. Roy was heavy. About fifty or sixty pounds overweight if he wanted to be honest with himself. He used to tell himself that it was just in his belly, but lately he had to admit that he could see it in his arms and in his face as well. He was a big guy, almost six foot two, but his weight had crept up to about two hundred and forty pounds when he knew he should be under two hundred. One hundred and eighty would be ideal.

As so many others had done, Roy had tried diets. He'd tried fruit diets, water diets, liquid protein diets and even fasting. Each time he lost weight, and he gained it back, and more. He really didn't believe that some new diet was the answer. When Roy first learned about

Alpha, he instantly saw its tremendous potential. "Diets are temporary, and as soon as I go off one, I always go back to the same old eating habits that necessitated the diet in the first place," Roy said. "It seems to me that by reprogramming my habits with Alpha, the changes I make will be permanent." By changing his eating habits, creating a physical exercise habit, and reprogramming his self image, Roy truly believed he could let go of the excess weight. He set about to do just that.

Roy closed his eyes, took a deep breath and imagined a peaceful place. Roy's peaceful place was the perfect vacuum of outer space. No light, no sounds, and no gravity; therefore no weight.

Roy loved to imagine that he was weightless and floating around in the peacefulness of the void. In the quiet of his mind, he asked himself a very basic question; "Why am I overweight?" He saw himself reading a book and eating a box of Cocoa Cereal.

He saw the two double cheeseburgers he had for lunch. He saw himself going to the refrigerator for beer after beer while watching TV. Inside himself, he knew that going to the refrigerator was the most exercise he was going to get all week. He saw himself as a fat person who was always eating much more food than he really needed to eat, and he saw himself as a lazy person who sat around most of the time and never really exercised at all. Roy knew what the problem was. It was time to wake up and work on the solution. Roy thought about what he had to do. "If I bring it right down to the basics," he thought, "it's about eating right and eating less food less often. I'll choose to order less at restaurants, and leave some on my plate. I'll choose to prepare smaller portions for myself at home. Mostly," he thought, "it's about eating right. After all those weight loss programs and diet books, I think I know what eating right means. In fact, I think almost everybody in America knows what eating right means. Not very many do it though.

"Well, I for one am going to be one who uses what I know. I know that much less meat and more whole grains, fruits, and vegetables would be best. I'll munch on carrots and celery more often, and make dessert a special occasional treat. I'll eat slower, take smaller bites, and chew my food better before I swallow. I'll choose to eat the right foods in the right way to achieve my ideal weight. No matter how correctly I eat, there is no way I can release as much weight as I need, unless I get regular exercise. I'm not much of an athlete, but one thing I know I can do is walk, and that's what I'm going to do. I'll start with a brisk ten-minute walk each day. Then I'll build it up to twenty minutes, and maybe later to twenty minutes twice a day. That will get my blood pumping and increase my metabolic rate so I can burn up those calories.

"Another thing I need to do while releasing the weight is to change my physical self image. I'll imagine myself at one hundred and eighty pounds, looking fit, trim, healthy and attractive. I'll imagine how incredibly wonderful it is to be so light and so free, and how very, very proud of myself I am for creating it. I understand that in Alpha, passion, is the key." So Roy went back to his peaceful place, to the feeling of floating weightless in outer space. As he relaxed, he visualized himself standing in front of a full-length mirror. The reflection that looked back at him was a fit, trim, one hundred and eighty pound hunk named Roy, who looked great and felt even better. He stood proud and tall, and his clothes fit him like a glove.

He was proud of his trim waistline, and of the muscle tone he could feel in his arms and legs. He was pleased with the way he looked from the top of his head to the tips of his toes. He then imagined himself at restaurants ordering a smaller portion than he used to, and eating it much more slowly. He even imagined that he left a little on the plate and found it easy to say "no thank you" when the dessert tray rolled by. Eating was a much more relaxed experience. He finished eating when he was no longer hungry, which came he soon discovered, way before he was full.

He imagined that he was at home, preparing a meal for himself. He noticed the smaller size of the portion that he was preparing. After dinner he visualized himself reading a book and munching on a stalk of celery. He pretended that he felt as if he really had his eating habits under control. Roy imagined himself walking briskly for ten and then twenty minutes a day. He saw himself walking faster everywhere he went, and sometimes passing up the elevator and taking the stairs. He imagined that he had more energy and every day he got closer to his trim and fit body, and his ideal weight. Averaging one or two pounds a week, it took Roy almost a year to reach his ideal weight. There were some weeks with no visible progress, then suddenly a few more pounds would drop off. Over the year Roy increased his exercise program to include a few pushups, and a few sit-ups, and eventually regular tennis. Roy stuck to it, and though it took a while, he understood that it was much healthier to release the weight gradually and that by doing this way, he would create a new set of habits. He knew that with these new eating and exercise habits, he need never put the weight back on again. In fact, six years later, he still hadn't.

Habits are often wonderful things. They free us up so that we can be inventive and creative. It would be difficult (if not impossible) to function without habits. Imagine having to decide which direction to go next with the toothbrush or which foot to use next when you are walking. For the most part, habits give us a lot of freedom. Habits are things that happen automatically.

We could look at the body's autonomic processes, such as heartbeat or breathing, as habits. We could say that it is by habit that we know how to form our mouths in certain ways to pronounce tens of thousands of words. By habit, we can easily remember how to return to any place where we've frequently been.

Good habits make life easy. Bad habits can wreck all the best laid plans for success. Breaking habits can be easy or difficult depending on the longevity and the intensity of the habit. The habits that are the most intense are called addictions. The intensity is determined by the number of times that you have repeated the habit and the volume of emotional amplitude you felt with each repetition. Habits create the condition where it is easier and easier to do something, and harder and harder to not do it. Perhaps the best way to break a habit is to create a new habit to take its place. Imagine that you are acting out the habitual behavior. Get in touch with what you were doing just before you began this habitual behavior. In this way, you can find the thing that triggers the habit.

When you identify the trigger of the habit, you can use that same trigger to program yourself to respond in a new way. Breaking habits often isn't so much an issue of not doing something as it is an issue of doing something else instead.

Quitting Smoking

Close your eyes, take a deep breath, and imagine your peaceful place. Make this quiet peaceful place you've chosen seem as real as you can. Imagine that off in the distance you see someone light up a cigarette. For an instant, you desire to have one, as you remember back to when you used to be a smoker. Instantly a very powerful feeling washes over your whole body. A warm flush of excitement rushes through you as you remember that you've quit, and you feel so proud of yourself for quitting. Every time you even think of smoking, you feel that rush of intense pride in yourself for quitting wash over you. That feeling of pride in your wonderful accomplishment brings you every bit of the satisfaction you desire. Feel an intense burst of pride. Whenever it feels comfortable for you, take a deep breath, open your eyes, come wide awake. Then get yourself up and with passion, take your next action step.

Releasing Excess Pounds

Close your eyes, take a deep breath, and imagine your peaceful place. Make this quiet peaceful place you've chosen seem as real as you can. Imagine yourself sitting down to eat a meal. Notice that you are eating a little bit slower than you used to and also notice that you have put a smaller portion of food on your plate. Be aware that you have chosen to eat the kind of food that you know is right for you. Now imagine standing in front of a full length mirror and seeing your reflection looking fit and trim. Get in touch with how wonderful it feels to be in such great shape. Next, imagine yourself doing some enjoyable form of exercise and imagine that you feel the physical exertion in your body. Intensify the wonderful feelings of physical fitness and excellent overall health. Whenever it feels comfortable for you, take a deep breath, open your eyes, come wide awake. Then get yourself up and with passion, take your next action step.

Procrastination

Close your eyes, take a deep breath, and imagine your peaceful place. Make this quiet peaceful place you've chosen seem as real as you can. Imagine the thought of getting started early on some important project. Notice how it feels to imagine working on this project feeling as if you have all the time in the world. Get in touch with how much better the work that you do is under these ideal circumstances. Think about what rewards might come your way because of the increased quality of your work. Feel how it feels to receive those rewards. Every time you even begin to think of procrastinating, the powerful thought of those rewards for starting early come into your mind. Whenever it feels comfortable for you, take a deep breath, open your eyes, come wide awake. Then get yourself up and with passion, take your next action step.

Listening

Close your eyes, take a deep breath, and imagine your peaceful place. Make this quiet peaceful place you've chosen seem as real as you can. Imagine that you are in a situation which calls for you really to listen to someone who has something very important to say to you. Notice how much easier it is to listen than it ever was before. Observe yourself feeding back to the person that you are listening to what you just heard. Listen to their comments of appreciation for your excellent listening skills. Feel proud of yourself for developing such a wonderful ability to listen and pay attention. Imagine all the different ways that this ability will benefit you in the future, and get in touch with how that feels. Whenever it feels comfortable for you, take a deep breath, open your eyes, come wide awake. Then get yourself up and with passion, take your next action step.

Controlling Your Temper

Close your eyes, take a deep breath, and imagine your peaceful place. Make this quiet peaceful place you've chosen seem as real as you can. Imagine a situation where in the past you would have felt angry and lost your temper. Notice where you are and who you are with. Get in touch with the changes that happen inside you. Now imagine a similar situation in the future, but imagine that this time you get angry but are able to keep control. Your breathing stays regular and your body becomes less tense. Notice how proud of yourself you are for holding your temper and for staying in control. Imagine releasing the anger in a more appropriate way. Listen to other people compliment you on your great self control. Feel the pride welling up inside for truly being in charge of your life. Whenever it feels comfortable for you, take a deep breath, open your eyes, come wide awake. Then get yourself up and with passion, take your next action step.

Releasing Stress

"What can I do," said BrainMind, "about stress?"

And HeartMind replied, "We can change it, rearrange it, we can slow it all down. Float gently with the current, not struggle or drown. The key is the thought, we can slow down our mind and when searching for peace, it's peace we will find. If we look for it inside, we'll find it will appear more and more on the planet, year after year."

Experiencing too much stress, tension, and anxiety, in the High Beta State, causes the filter (the reticular activating system) to shut down between our minds, and we lose access to our creativity, imagination, intelligence, and memory. Stress builds in our lives based on what's going on, and on how we deal with it. The secret is not to live less stressful lives. It is to consistently release your stress through the course of each day.

Based on one of the most powerful laws of physics (an object in motion tends to stay in motion in the direction that it is moving), going to your peaceful place begins the process of relaxation, that continues even after you open your eyes and go back about your business. The relaxation continues until the next stressful thing happens, which gets your stress levels moving back in the other direction again.

A great metaphor is weight lifting. You can pick up a big heavy piece of metal and you can lift it for a while, but after a while longer, it starts to get hard to do. After a little while longer, it gets to the point where you can not do one more.

No matter how much will power, determination, or intention you have, you simply can not do one more. But put the weight down and let the arm rest for just a few moments, and now you can do some more. It's the same thing with your immune system and your ability to handle stress. Put down all of the tension, all of the anxiety, all of the problems, for a just few moments and you can quickly become revitalized and reinvigorated. Go frequently to your peaceful place, and simply let your stress go.

Peter was a nervous wreck. His sales were way down, his one kid was failing high school, and his other kid was down with the flu. His car was in the shop, again, and the rental car he was driving had a funny rattling noise under the hood, that was making him very uncomfortable. On top of all that it was starting to rain, and he was going to be late for work. His fingers were clamped tightly on the steering wheel and he felt the muscles in his legs begin to stiffen up. Work was really stressful, and home was really stressful and there was no escape from it while driving in traffic in the rain. Peter found no escape from the stresses in his life except when he was asleep. He was getting six or seven hours of restless sleep each night, virtually no rest during the day, and it just didn't seem to be enough. Peter knew he had to do something significant very soon because the quality of his life was deteriorating fast. When he was introduced to Alpha he thought it just might offer him the solution. When he first tried it, Peter closed his eyes and took a deep breath. He spent a few moments attempting to imagine a peaceful place but nothing was coming to mind. Then Peter got distracted by a car going by outside, and he started to think about how much money he had spent in the last year on fixing his stupid car. Needless to say, his peaceful place was not in sight.

"At first I couldn't come up with any kind of peaceful place for the life of me, and when I finally did, I kept thinking of everything else except that. I stuck with it though, and just kept on getting back to that place. Eventually, it started to come easily.

"Whenever I was distracted by outside sounds or noises, I just let them go and returned to my place of peace. Whenever I was distracted by my own thoughts about bills or work, or whatever, I would tell myself a time when I would think about them, and then I would let them go and get back to my peaceful place. For my place, I picked a memory I had of Grandpa's farm. I was lying up in the hayloft in the barn on a beautiful spring day. I had just finished one of Grandma's incredible breakfasts, and I was lying there in the barn, with the smell of fresh cut hay all around me. It is one of my favorite memories.

"From that peaceful place I asked myself, how do I deal with all the stress in my life? This is what came to me as the answer. The thought was that my mind is like a tea kettle, and it is boiling and full of steam. I need to let the steam out, a little bit at a time, and I need to do it all day long. I realized that I don't have all that much stress—no more than millions of other people. It's just in the way that I handle it, or more accurately don't handle it. No one situation is beyond my control, it's just that when you put them all together, they feel pretty overwhelming. The solution, I realized, is to handle one thing at a time. After doing that one thing, then it's time to take a minute or so to relax and let go of all the stress, all of the physical tension and emotional anxiety. Just by imagining that scene on my grandparents farm, for a minute or so each time, I let my body and my mind relax. This leaves me better equipped to be the best I can be next time."

In the most intense forms of stress, such as life threatening situations, we have a fight or flight response. Less frequently we have a freeze or faint response. These responses are automatic and originate in the very core of our brain. The relative importance of any given situation determines the intensity of the response. Stress motivates and stimulates us into action. Without stress, we might not even get out of bed in the morning.

Stress allows us to respond to life. It is our response to those things that we encounter in life that really matter. Stress can push us forward towards life's greatest successes. Too much stress can also debilitate us. Stress related illness (dis-ease) is our number one killer. Many people relate well to stress and perform their best under pressure. Some professional athletes and many other entertainers need the performance anxiety to do their best. Some people rarely perform at their best unless they are under pressure. Other people tend to choke under pressure. The harder they try the harder it becomes.

Responding negatively to stress results in creating tension and anxiety. Stress affects each of us in different ways. Two people may experience the same stressful situation, but they might respond in their own unique and individual ways. When "the game is on the line" some do better, some worse.

The ability to perform under pressure is the key to success in many areas of life. Those who consistently do better under pressure reap life's rewards, while those who consistently do worse under pressure learn to avoid it. They rarely reach prominence in any field that involves performance or competition. It is not so much the nature of the stress that matters as much as it is the way that you respond to it. Usually we react out of habit. We can instead reprogram and use the pressure to motivate us to do our best in those situations that matter the most.

Alpha can become your most effective technique for getting rid of excess tension and anxiety that you carry in your mind and in your body. Whenever you face a task, you automatically build up the stress that you need to face that task. All too often, however, we are still carrying the stress left over from our previous task. We move on to the next stressful situation having not released the stress we built to face the last one. Alpha can become the hole in the top of the tea kettle of life. It is a way to release excess stress before there is a chance for it to accumulate and become potentially dangerous. DIS-EASE is one result of failing effectively to handle the stresses of life. It is essential to spend some of our time at ease, in order to avoid dis-ease. It doesn't take a lot of time at ease to counteract the negative effects of stress. What it takes is a lot of times. Lots of repetitions of closing our eyes, taking a deep breath, and going to the state of Focused Passion.

Release

Close your eyes, take a deep breath, and imagine your peaceful place. Make this quiet peaceful place you've chosen seem as real as you can. Tune into your physical body and notice which areas seem to be holding the most stress, both as physical tension and as emotional anxiety. Imagine that the tension and anxiety in your body is being gently released through an imaginary release valve, located in some convenient part of your body as you feel your body begin to relax. Imagine the stress as a particular color, and watch as that color begins to fade away. Imagine the stress as a particular sound that seems to become quieter and quieter as it fades off into the distance. Tension is replaced by relaxation. Whenever it feels comfortable for you, take a deep breath, open your eyes, come wide awake. Then get yourself up and—with passion—take your next action step.

Cool Down

Close your eyes, take a deep breath, and imagine your peaceful place. Make this quiet peaceful place you've chosen seem as real as you can. Imagine that the tension and anxiety in your body is represented by a feeling of warmth deep down inside. Begin to pretend that some of the heat is being comfortably released through your skin. For a few moments imagine that your body feels warmer and warmer and then feel yourself begin to cool down. Pretend that your body begins to feel cooler and cooler until you have comfortably released much of your stress. Imagine that your body temperature is returning to normal and feel a sense of calmness and comfort throughout your entire body. Whenever it feels comfortable for you, take a deep breath, open your eyes, come wide awake. Then get yourself up and with passion, take your next action step.

Wash Away

Close your eyes, take a deep breath, and imagine your peaceful place. Make this quiet peaceful place you've chosen seem as real as you can. Get in touch with the areas of your body where you seem to be holding on to tension and anxiety. Imagine that the tension and anxiety in your body could (like oil) come through the sweat glands and out of the pores in your skin. Pretend that you are stepping into a shower in order to wash away all of your excess stress. Imagine covering your entire body with a very special kind of soap. Pretend that the soap not only leaves you very clean but that it has special stress reducing qualities as well. As you rinse this special soap off of your body, feel all the excess tension and anxiety in your body wash away and flow down the drain. Whenever it feels comfortable for you, take a deep breath, open your eyes, come wide awake. Then get yourself up and with passion, take your next action step.

Grounding

Close your eyes, take a deep breath, and imagine your peaceful place. Make this quiet peaceful place you've chosen seem as real as you can. Imagine that you are standing barefoot in thick oozing mud. Feel the mud squish between your toes and cover up your feet. Imagine that your feet slowly sink three inches into the mud. Get the feeling that the earth itself is drawing out of you all the excess tension and anxiety. Like the ground on a battery all the excess tension and anxiety in your body is harmlessly discharged into the earth. Feel yourself relaxing and releasing more and more as all of the excess stress drains away through the mud, transforming to positive energy as it flows down into the planet. Feel this relaxation and stress reduction continue moving down and out of your feet. Whenever it feels comfortable for you, take a deep breath, open your eyes, come wide awake. Then get yourself up and with passion, take your next action step.

Create The Future

Close your eyes, take a deep breath, and imagine your peaceful place. Make this quiet peaceful place you've chosen seem as real as you can. Imagine a future situation or circumstance that you desire a great deal; yet, at the same time it seems a little frightening to you. Pretend that you handle the situation with perfect confidence. Notice how the feelings of fear transform into feelings of excitement. Become aware of the feelings of success that come over you with this accomplishment. Replay this wonderful scene over and over in your mind. Feel those powerful feelings of accomplishment increase for a few moments. Notice where in your body you feel these feelings the most. Whenever it feels comfortable for you, take a deep breath, open your eyes, come wide awake. Then get yourself up and with passion, take your next action step.

Repair The Past

Close your eyes, take a deep breath, and imagine your peaceful place. Make this quiet peaceful place you've chosen seem as real as you can. Remember a past situation or circumstance that you still think about; that caused you a lot of tension and anxiety. Pretend instead that you handled the situation with perfect confidence. Notice how the feelings of negativity transform into feelings of positively. Become aware of the feelings of success that come over you with this recreated accomplishment. Replay this new scene over and over in your mind. Feel those powerful feelings of success and accomplishment increase for a few moments. Notice where in your body you feel these powerful feelings the most. Whenever it feels comfortable for you, take a deep breath, open your eyes, come wide awake.

Solving Problems

"Tell me," said BrainMind, "about solving problems."
HeartMind replied:
"When it comes to solving problems, it is easier to do
When it's someone else's problem, not happening to you
And sometimes solving problems, is so easy that it seems
The answers to our problems come to us in our dreams
Other times the more we try, the more we draw a blank
As if someone froze the assets, inside our memory bank
There is always a solution, always some way to explain
Just block out the distractions and utilize our brain
Relax and go to Alpha, in doing this you'll find
Problems have solutions, to be found inside our mind."

Stan had a problem. As the founder and president of a small electronics manufacturing company, Stan was faced with an important decision. Ted, his long time executive vice president and key right hand man, had decided to retire. Ted was only fifty-five and Stan had expected to have him around for at least another five or ten years. Sitting at his desk, Stan pondered the problem of who would replace Ted. "The two obvious options," thought Stan, "are to promote someone from within the company, or to go outside and hire someone new. The third option would be whatever option I haven't thought of yet.

"From inside the company it would have to be one of the other two vice presidents. It would be either Robert, the VP of Manufacturing, or Sandra, the VP of Sales." The problem with Robert is, I don't think he's ready yet. After all, he is only twenty-six years old, and although he is a wizard with electronics, he just hasn't learned all of the ins and outs of the business world yet.

If Ted had waited a few more years before retiring, no question, Robert would be my choice, but I'm just not sure that he's ready. "Sandra, on the other hand, could do the job, but I'd hate to lose her as VP of sales. She is by far the best salesperson that I have ever worked with in all my years in the business."

"If I promote Sandra to executive vice president she would be so wrapped up in the corporate paperwork that she would be lost to the field. Besides, Sandra loves the customers. She'd get bored being stuck behind a desk.

I want to avoid the Peter Principle here. Just because she is doing great at sales, doesn't mean I should promote her to a job that she might not like and might not do as well." Stan sat back in his chair and continued to explore his options.

"I could go outside and bring in someone new. Someone with a background in both sales and manufacturing. The problem there is that it is hard for some people to adjust to a new boss, and there may be some hard feelings.

I'm especially concerned with how Robert would take it. Robert's the one I want to run this place for me after I retire. I'm afraid that if I hire someone from outside, instead of promoting him, he might just go somewhere else. The truth is that I need Robert a whole lot more than he needs me. With his knowledge and skills and talent, he could work almost anywhere on the planet." Stan reviewed his options. "Sandra could do it, but I'd hate to lose her from sales. Robert could do it but maybe not yet. I could go outside and get somebody else, but then I might lose Robert. No matter which way I go, it's more work for me, training someone for the job. This comes just at the time when I was starting to cut back on my hours. I was really looking forward to taking more and more time off, leading up to retiring in a few years. With Ted retiring early, it looks as though I'm back to the old drawing board with that plan.

I wonder if there are any other ways of handling this situation that I haven't seen yet? This is the time," Stan thought, "to put Alpha to work. I am going to tap into my creative potential." Stan closed his eyes, took a deep breath, and imagined his peaceful place. Stan's peaceful place was at the top of Half Dome Mountain in Yosemite National Park. He was looking across the valley at the massive hunk of granite known as El Capitan. He felt the cool crisp wind on his cheeks and a sense of joyous exhilaration in his heart. Stan suggested to himself that he would have access to his intelligence, creativity and intuition, in solving the problem of whom to choose. He asked himself, "What other options are there to consider when searching for the best solution to a problem?" His mind's screen was blank for a just a few moments and then a full color picture began to appear. What he saw, floating in the air, was a chart of the corporate ladder. Starting with himself on the top, Ted (who was retiring) below him, with Robert and Sandra below Ted.

Stan: Pres.
$200,000

Ted: Exec. VP (Retired)
$150,000

Robert: VP MFG   ## Sandra: VP Sales
$100,000   ## $100,000

In Stan's mind, the old chart began drifting over to the left of his vision. From his right, a new chart began to appear.

Stan: Chairman
$200,000

Robert: Chief Exec.
$125,000

Sandra: Chief Finc.
$125,000

New Asst. VP MFG
$50,000

New Asst. VP Sales
$50,000

Stan took a deep breath and brought himself back to awake. He wrote down what he saw. "What a great solution," he thought. "I could take Ted's job, and even a little of my job, and divide it up between Robert and Sandra. They each could do half of Ted's job, and some key parts of their old jobs, and they can each hire an assistant to do the rest. Sandra stays involved in sales, but also expands into other financial areas, and Robert stays focused on electronics, but also gets a taste of running the company with Sandra as his partner.

"An excellent solution and if I hadn't opened my mind with Alpha, I might never have seen it. All I was thinking was, one person was leaving and one person must take his place. When I relaxed into Alpha, I could see that I wasn't limited to that one way of doing it. I found a way where everybody wins and nobody loses, and that is the best way that there is to solve a problem."

Solving problems is an exercise in creativity. The point is not to create a life with no problems, but rather to become a better and better problem solver.

As we leave the Industrial Age and move into the Information Age there is a need to develop different skills. In this new age, the two most important skills become creativity and problem solving, making things up, and figuring things out. In the past, many people had very similar jobs—working in factories on the assembly line. In the future, specialization is becoming more and more prevalent; and in the office, everyone is doing something different.

We can no longer depend on the same old answers because we are creating brand new problems. The key to the future of our civilization involves creativity and problem solving. How we experience our problems is a more significant factor in our happiness than are the specific problems that we experience. Instead of complaining and worrying, we can learn to see our problems as creative opportunities that give us the chance to grow and improve. We can take on our problems as puzzles to be solved, or as challenges to be overcome.

When we get into stressful Beta States, the filter (the reticular activating system) closes down, denying us access to higher intelligence, memory and creativity. By utilizing the Alpha State you get in touch with your problem solving capabilities.

With the filter open, you can use your imagination to go beyond what you know into all that could be. Often it is difficult to solve our problems because we can't clearly see the problem for what it truly is. This is the "you can't see the forest for the trees" syndrome.

We get caught up in the emotions and sometimes seem to blow the problem out of all proportion. Sometimes it serves to take an alternate perception and see the problem in a different way. Step outside the problem and change your perception, and the problem seems to change as well. You could imagine that the problem belongs to someone else. If this were true, what kind of advice would you give him? What would you say that his first step could be? How would you help to motivate him and get him going? What resources would you suggest he use? How could you help him be confident of his process and his ultimate success?

You could pretend that the problem is already solved. Think backwards from the solution to the first step. Remember what you did. Where were you when you figured it out. Sometimes we can solve a problem simply by realizing that it is not really a problem at all. Many problems can be seen in a positive light as creative opportunities. For every problem there are solutions. Some are better than others. One of the most limiting forms of thinking is to assume that there is only one right answer to your problem. This rigid and restrictive thinking process comes from stress and is reinforced in school. High stress creates a fight or flight response and an either/or mentality. Right or wrong, good or bad, this mentality limits or thinking. When we only see either/ or, we do not get a chance to explore neither or both. The belief in only one right answer seriously inhibits creativity. We must break out of that mold in order to be truly effective problem solvers. If you relax your mind and use your imagination and your creativity you will find unlimited resources at your disposal. Almost all of the great problems that have ever been solved have had their solutions begin in some woman's or some man's daydream.

Giving It Away

Close your eyes, take a deep breath, and imagine your peaceful place. Make this quiet peaceful place you've chosen seem as real as you can. Imagine that the problem that you have belongs instead to someone else. Pretend that you are working with this person in order to help him solve it. Observe yourself as you help him solve his problem. Be aware of the creativity and confidence to which you have access. Make note of the advice that you give him and how your confidence shows through in the process. Imagine the step-by-step method that you employ on his behalf. Feel the gratitude and appreciation that he gives you for your help. Get in touch with how easy it is to help someone with a problem. Whenever it feels comfortable for you, take a deep breath, open your eyes, come wide awake. Then get yourself up and with passion, take your next action step.

It's All Over

Close your eyes, take a deep breath, and imagine your peaceful place. Make this quiet peaceful place you've chosen seem as real as you can. Imagine that the problem that you have had already been solved sometime in the recent past. Get in touch with how it feels now that it's over. Imagine the exact moment when you realized that you had done it. Remember back to how the solution came to mind. Remember where you were and exactly what you were doing at the time. Let your mind carefully review all of the steps that you took to come to this wonderful solution. Whenever it feels comfortable for you, take a deep breath, open your eyes, come wide awake. Then get yourself up and with passion, take your next action step.

Reverse The Problem

Close your eyes, take a deep breath, and imagine your peaceful place. Make this quiet peaceful place you've chosen seem as real as you can. Imagine the problem that you are facing in great detail. Now imagine that instead of the problem that you've had, you now have in its place, a problem that is the reverse of your original problem. See this problem in great detail. Imagine step by step exactly what you need to do to solve this reverse problem. After you do this, reverse your solution and see what insights you get that will assist you in solving the real problem. Feel confident that with these insight you have what you need to help you solve your true problem. Whenever it feels comfortable for you, take a deep breath, open your eyes, come wide awake. Then get yourself up and with passion, take your next action step.

Problem-Solving Pal

Close your eyes, take a deep breath, and imagine your peaceful place. Make this quiet peaceful place you've chosen seem as real as you can. Imagine that sitting next to you is your problem solving pal. It can be a male or a female, adult or child, human or alien being. Imagine what this problem-solving pal looks like. A special make-believe friend who knows you well and yet can take an objective viewpoint when you are discussing your problems. Imagine explaining your problem to your problem solving pal in great detail. Notice how attentive your pal is while listening to you explain the circumstances. Pretend that your pal begins to offer some ideas that lead you to potential solutions. Listen to these words of wisdom and remember them well. Whenever it feels comfortable for you, take a deep breath, open your eyes, come wide awake. Then get yourself up and with passion, take your next action step.

The Book Of Solutions

Close your eyes, take a deep breath, and imagine your peaceful place. Make this quiet peaceful place you've chosen seem as real as you can. Imagine that you have in your possession a very important book. This is the only existing copy in the world of this most amazing book. You are holding in your hands the Book of Solutions. Imagine what this book looks like and how it feels in your hands. When you open this book to any page that you choose, any solution to any problem can be found. Imagine looking up solutions to your problems, the problems of your friends and loved ones, and the problems of the whole planet. Be very thankful that this wonderful book has been put into your hands for safekeeping. Feel the power for good for all humankind that this book allows you to possess. Whenever it feels comfortable for you, take a deep breath, open your eyes, come wide awake. Then get yourself up and with passion, take your next action step

Pain Control and Healing

"How," asked BrainMind, "can we work together to control our pain and accelerate our healing?"

HeartMind replied, "Most of what you feel as pain, is not in the place you feel it. It is a signal that I amplify so that we can better heal it. I make you pay attention as I make you focus in. That is when the pain control and healing can begin."

Jenny knew she had a wonderful life. Married to a great husband, raised three wonderful, kids, and then found a fulfilling career. The only problem was, she was so often in pain. Sometimes it wasn't too bad and she could, almost, ignore it. Other times though; she didn't even want to think about some of those other times. She had been in an accident late last year and her injured back and neck had not fully recovered. She had some not so bad days, and some real terrible days, when it came to pain. She knew she could take pain killing drugs, and once in a while, when it got real bad, she would.

But she didn't want to live like that, half in and half out of reality. She couldn't really function well at all on the medication. She was talking to her Pharmacist one afternoon about not wanting to use the pills so much. The Pharmacist told Jenny a little about Alpha, and how she could use the power of her mind to stop the pain from growing stronger, and maybe even to make the pain fade completely away. He gave her a tape to listen to that would guide her into the Alpha State and teach her how to return to Alpha whenever she wished. When she went home she listened to the tape. She learned how to go to Alpha. She closed her eyes, and went to her peaceful place, a place where she was peacefully floating in a liquid world, weightless and totally free of pain.

Sometimes she just went to Alpha for a few moments or so, but sometimes she'd go for half an hour. She found that using Alpha as early as possible, before the pain had a chance to build, was the most effective way to control it, but anytime she used Alpha, she took away a lot of the pain. As the weeks went by she was getting better and better with Alpha, and using the medication less and less. She had occasional bad days but the Alpha made it easier, and there were a lot more pain free days where it was easy to remember that she had a really great life.

Only a small part of the pain we feel in the actual tactile receptor sites, that is, in the place we feel it. Most of the pain we feel, is Heart-Mind amplifying the signal to get BrainMind's attention. When you pay attention to pain it can then begin to diminish. It has now successfully done it's job of bringing your attention to the site of the injury.

By paying complete attention to the pain, it fades away sooner. If you are angry that you hurt yourself, that emotion of anger is now in competition with the pain, to get your attention. Focus BrainMind on the pain and HeartMind can make it fade away. Healing disease can also be accelerated by using Alpha. Focus on the imagining yourself empowering your immune system to beat that Cold Germ, or visualize yourself already healed, have totally wiped out that Flu Virus. Best yet, use the power of your minds to stay well. Sometime it works even better to go down to deep Alpha or light Theta to heal. First go to your peaceful place as usual, and then imagine yourself going deeper and deeper down. Remember if you go too deep you fall asleep.

Uncoloring The Pain

Close your eyes, take a deep breath, and imagine your peaceful place. Make this quiet peaceful place you've chosen seem as real as you can. Imagine the pain you experience as having a color Imagine the color in vivid detail. Imagine that you are making the pain fade by making the color fade. Automatically as you relax in your peaceful place and imagine the color fading, the pain fades as well. The more the color fades the more the pain fades until the last traces of the lightest version of that color fade away, and the pain fades with it. Whenever it feels comfortable for you, take a deep breath, open your eyes, come wide awake.

Shrinking The Pain

Close your eyes, take a deep breath, and imagine your peaceful place. Make this quiet peaceful place you've chosen seem as real as you can. Imagine the pain you experience as having a size and a shape. Imagine the size and shape in vivid detail. Imagine that you are making the pain fade by making the size shrink, and the shape collapse. Automatically as you relax in your peaceful place and imagine the size shrinking, and the shape collapsing, the pain shrinks as well. The more it shrinks, the more the pain fades until the smallest fades away, and the pain fades with it. Whenever it feels comfortable for you, take a deep breath, open your eyes, come wide awake.

Smoothing The Pain

Close your eyes, take a deep breath, and imagine your peaceful place. Make this quiet peaceful place you've chosen seem as real as you can. Imagine the pain you experience as having a texture and feel to it. Imagine the texture in vivid detail. Imagine that you are making the pain fade away by making the texture smooth out. Automatically as you relax in your peaceful place and imagine the texture smoothing out, the pain shrinks as well. The smoother it gets, the more the pain fades until even the smallest part of the pain fades away. Whenever it feels comfortable for you, take a deep breath, open your eyes, come wide awake.

Heating The Cold

Close your eyes, take a deep breath, and imagine your peaceful place. Make this quiet peaceful place you've chosen seem as real as you can. Imagine the cold that you are experiencing as having a cold temperature. Imagine the cold in vivid detail. Imagine that you are making the cold fade away by making the cold warmer. Automatically as you relax in your peaceful place and imagine the inner warmth, you imagine the cold shrinks as well. The warmer you get, the more the cold fades, until even the smallest part of the cold is gone. Whenever it feels comfortable for you, take a deep breath, open your eyes, come wide awake.

Inflating The Immune System

Close your eyes, take a deep breath, and imagine your peaceful place. Make this quiet peaceful place you've chosen seem as real as you can. Imagine your immune system, as if it were a beach ball that you are inflating. Imagine the beach ball in vivid detail. Imagine that you are making the beach ball inflate thus making your immune system stronger. Automatically as you relax in your peaceful place and imagine inflating your immune system, your immune system actually gets stronger. The fuller the beach ball gets, the stronger you feel, until you feel full. Whenever it feels comfortable for you, take a deep breath, open your eyes, come wide awake.

Water For Wellness

Close your eyes, take a deep breath, and imagine your peaceful place. Make this quiet peaceful place you've chosen seem as real as you can. Imagine the water you drink and experience it as having a texture and feel to it. Imagine that you are making the body heal by flowing healing water through it. Automatically as you drink water you get healthier. The more you drink, the more the water heals you until every part of you is fully hydrated. Imagine the healing power of the water every time you drink. Whenever it feels comfortable for you, take a deep breath, open your eyes, come wide awake.

Improving Memory

"How important," asked BrainMind, "is a good memory?"

"Of all the things that we possess, our memory's the very best. Of every single thing we own, memory's ours and ours alone. It's everything we've ever learned, it's all the lessons that we've earned. It's everything we've ever done, it's all the pain and all the fun. Our memory gives us special powers, its use can save us countless hours.

"Most times it tells us what to do, unless the circumstance is new. But once we've done it we can again, upon our memory we depend. To release our minds so we can be, creators of reality," replied HeartMind.

Bert was a pretty successful guy. He had a great wife, a couple of wonderful kids and a thriving law practice in West Los Angeles. But there was one thing that bugged him; he had the most difficult time remembering people's names. It wasn't everybody. He remembered his family of course, and he always remembered his clients. It was all the other people. Like the guy he played golf with that one time, or the couple he was introduced to at the party. He could remember everything about them, where they lived, what they did, how they looked, everything; except for their names. He was always able to get around it, which took more intelligence then remembering would have, but it bothered him a lot that he couldn't remember names. He knew he had a good memory. After all, he did pass the bar exam the first time out, but this name thing really got him. When Bert heard about Alpha he thought, "This might be just the thing. If it can help me remember people's names then it will be the find of a lifetime."

Bert closed his eyes and imagined a peaceful place. He imagined that he was snorkeling in the warm aquamarine waters of the Caribbean Ocean. Brilliant multi-colored fish swam by just inches out of reach. There was a wonderful sense of freedom that came with floating under the water. Then in Alpha, Bert asked himself a question. "Why has it been so difficult for me to remember people's names?" The answer came in his mind's eye in a sort of visualization.

Bert saw himself going up to the front door of a lovely home that he recognized belonged to Ken, a good friend of his. When he knocked on the door, Ken opened it and said, "Bert, it's great to see you, come in, come in." He walked Bert over to a group of four men and began to make introductions.

He said, "Bert, I want you to meet some other friends of mine, Bert I'd like you to meet, and then Ken rattled off four names. As he did this, Bert noticed that he wasn't paying attention to the names Ken was saying at all. All he was hearing, really loudly, in his mind was, "I'LL NEVER REMEMBER THEIR NAMES!" Bert woke himself up and thought about what he had seen. He realized that although he wasn't remembering names, it really wasn't his memory's fault. The names were never getting into his memory bank because he was blocking them out. He was doing this by thinking with so much passion, and certainty, "I'LL NEVER BE ABLE TO REMEMBER THEIR NAMES!"

The next thing that Bert did was go back to Alpha, to his underwater peaceful place, to do another Alpha process. This time he imagined the same scenario with a different ending. This time when Ken introduced the four men, he listened very carefully to their names, and even imagined something silly to help him remember.

Ken said, "Bert, I'd like you to meet Bill, (Bert imagined "PAID" stamped on Bill's forehead), Frank, (Bert imagined Frank had a frankfurter for a nose), John (Bert imagined a toilet flush as one of John's ears), and Harry (Bert imagined Harry had hair growing all over his body). Bert then imagined saying to the four men, "Bill, Frank, John, Harry, so nice to meet you," and then he imagined thinking, with great confidence "I KNOW I AM REMEMBERING THEIR NAMES AND IT FEELS GREAT!"

Next Bert imagined that it was some later date and he saw the four men at another occasion. He imagined walking right up to them and saying, "Bill, Frank, John, Harry, so nice to see you guys again." Bert was proud of himself for remembering, and he knew that from then on, he would easily remember people's names. With few exceptions, he was right.

Perhaps the most valuable thing that we possess is our memory. It allows us to learn from our mistakes and thus enables us to continue to grow. Its contents help to dictate the attitudes and behaviors that we utilize when we face the world. Your long-term memory is perfect. It is the bank, the permanent storage house for all the information that you have ever paid attention to. There are things that come into short term memory (usually only seconds long) and never make it into long-term permanent storage. If information gets into long term memory, you have it forever. However, your recall of that information can mess up sometimes. The problem is in recall, not in memory. We remember millions of things for every one thing that we forget. There are an un-limited number of ways to remember things and there are only two possible ways to forget.

One way that we forget things is called the "tip-of-the-tongue" syndrome. In this situation, under pressure, the brain produces High Beta Waves and the filter closes down, and the information comes up and hits the filter.

The harder you try to remember, the tighter the filter closes. It is only when you finally relax and move into Alpha, the state of Focused Passion, that the stress goes away, that the filter opens back up again.

The other way that we forget things is when we create a block to remembering. Often we do this by saying, "I have a terrible memory" and then agreeing with that suggestion. Blocks can be more specific such as, "I can never remember names" or "I'm terrible with dates." We also create blocks by thinking, "History is boring," or "Algebra puts me to sleep."

We often blame our memory when it is not our memory's fault. You begin to leave a meeting, you walk to the door, and then you say, "Oh, I forgot my briefcase." The truth is that you just remembered your briefcase, and really could have used the opportunity to say something positive about your memory. If we only pay attention to our memory when it fails, it is liable to fail just to get our attention. Compliment your memory at every opportunity. Whenever you remember anything difficult, or anything from a long time ago, make sure to say to yourself, "Good Memory." Whenever you see someone else exhibit a great memory, compliment them and think, me too. Your memory improves each and every time you reinforce it.

When someone else remembers to do something that you asked him to do, compliment him on their good memory. This reminds you that you have a wonderful memory too. We remember what we pay attention to. If, when we are introduced to people, make powerful associations, you are much more likely to remember the names.

Past Recollections

Close your eyes, take a deep breath, and imagine your peaceful place. Make this quiet peaceful place you've chosen seem as real as you can. Imagine a very special time from your past. Remember where you were and who, if anyone, was with you. Get in touch with what you were doing at the time. Remember exactly what you were seeing, hearing, smelling, touching, tasting and feeling at the time. Begin to realize just how wonderful your ability to remember things really is. Let your mind switch to another time, and then another. Realize that you have thousands and thousands of these passionate times stored up inside you. Whenever it feels comfortable for you, take a deep breath, open your eyes, come wide awake. Then get yourself up and with passion, take your next action step.

Keys To Recall

Close your eyes, take a deep breath, and imagine your peaceful place. Make this quiet peaceful place you've chosen seem as real as you can. Imagine that you are returning home from being out on an errand. Imagine taking your keys and setting them down somewhere in your house. As you put them down, imagine that, for just a moment, you stare at that spot and inside your mind you yell "KEYS." When it is time to leave again, notice how easy it is to remember where you put your keys. Realize that with this simple technique you will always be able to remember where you put your keys as well as anything else you wish to be able to locate. Think of other things that this technique will assist you with. Whenever it feels comfortable for you, take a deep breath, open your eyes, come wide awake. Then get yourself up and with passion, take your next action step.

I Just Remembered

Close your eyes, take a deep breath, and imagine your peaceful place. Make this quiet peaceful place you've chosen seem as real as you can. Imagine a situation where in the past you would have said "I forgot (something)." Imagine another situation and yet another. Begin to realize just how often you used to say those words, "I forgot." Imagine that instead from this moment on you find yourself saying, "I just remembered (something)." Feel really proud of yourself because you realize that you have taken a major step toward improving your recall ability. Hear yourself saying over and over, "I just remembered," "I just remembered." Feel the pride inside yourself for making this all important change in your language and your memory. Whenever it feels comfortable for you, take a deep breath, open your eyes, come wide awake. Then get yourself up and with passion, take your next action step.

Memory Test

Close your eyes, take a deep breath, and imagine your peaceful place. Make this quiet peaceful place you've chosen seem as real as you can.

Imagine that you are taking a test. This test measures how well you remember information that you have studied. In your imagination, step outside yourself and, from a distance, observe yourself taking the test. Watch as your pen moves quickly across the answer sheet. Notice the smile on your face and the twinkle in your eye. Get the sense that you are remembering everything. See yourself finish and watch as you check to be sure that your answers are correct. Notice how you nod and smile with each correct answer that you check. Get in touch with how it feels to be a great test taker. Enjoy that feeling of confidence and competence as you count yourself from zero to five and return to the present.

Accelerated Reading

"What does reading," asked BrainMind, "feel like to you?"
"It is like a voyage to elsewhere, a journey beyond
A feeling of oneness, a synergy bond
A universe uncovered, a galaxy explored
A varied chase thru time and space never getting bored
To unicorns' and dragons' homes,
Where mystery and magic dwell,
To utopias and heavens and to the nether depths of hell
From the hobbit's shire to the caveman's fire,
To space ships and walks on the moon
From the north pole in December to the amazon in June
To dinosaurs, distant shores, spirits, ghosts and ghouls
From the wisdom of ancients to the folly of fools
The universe is here for us, if we only take a look
And the magic does begin each time we open up a book," replied HeartMind.

Earl was the General Manager of the new technologies division of a major defense contractor. He had put his staff of fifty top engineers through the best time management training that money could buy. They found that the training allowed them to be much more productive. They all agreed, that there was still one major bottleneck that slowed the whole process down, and that was how much they had to read, and how long it took to read it. Earl said, "No matter how organized we were, it still seemed to take forever to get through all of the letters, and memos, and contracts, and proposals, and articles, and manuals, and books. Most of his staff spent at least forty hours every month, (2 hours per day) reading, but some engineers averaged as much as one hundred hours per month (5 hours per day). That's a big chunk of their time.

Earl saw the need for an accelerated reading program, but he was also very wary. He didn't trust those trainings that promised better comprehension at ten or twenty thousand words per minute. He knew them for what they were. Basically, you give up reading and instead skim through the material as fast as you can and see how much you get. This is a good way to see if you want to read something or not, but it is no substitute for reading. What Earl wanted was a program that could take his staff of technical engineers from the 150 *to* 300 words per minute range up into the 450 *to* 1,200 words per minute range, with increased comprehension. He found out that this could be accomplished with Alpha.

At an accelerated learning program—that featured Alpha Techniques—Earl's staff accomplished their mission. They programmed their eyes to read a third of a line at a time. This is more than three times the amount that they used to perceive in every individual focus. This alone more than tripled the average reading speed. They practiced eye exercises to both loosen and strengthen their eye muscles. They also learned to reprogram their posture, their breathing, the way they held the book and turned pages, facial expressions, and levels of concentration and interest in the material. They reprogrammed every aspect of the way they read. After the accelerated learning seminar, focused on accelerated reading through Alpha, the average reading speed of Earl's engineers went from 199 words per minute to 667 words per minute with a dramatic increase in comprehension. What only days earlier had taken the average person two hours a day to read, they could now read in thirty-five to forty minutes. One hundred hours a month became thirty-five hours a month or fewer. Earl says frequently that accelerated reading through Alpha was an all time great investment for his staff.

Magic Book

Close your eyes, take a deep breath, and imagine your a peaceful place. Make this quiet peaceful place you've chosen seem as real as you can. Imagine that your magic book is in this place. Pretend that this book has magical properties. It can feed the hungry, or heal the sick, or end war for all time. Imagine that you LOVE this book, as much or more than you have ever loved anything. Hold this magic book in your hands. Realize the amazing treasure that it really is. This book has the power to change the way that you read forever. This book can help you learn to be excited and interested in everything that you read. Whenever it feels comfortable for you, take a deep breath, open your eyes, come wide awake. Then get yourself up and with passion, take your next action step.

Read With Speed

Close your eyes, take a deep breath, and imagine your peaceful place. Make this quiet peaceful place you've chosen seem as real as you can. Imagine that you are about to read a wonderful book. Imagine that before you read you scan the material very, very quickly. You move your eyes over the material at a rate far beyond your reading speed. Faster and faster you exercise your eyes, preparing them to read. When you finish and actually begin to read, you notice that you are reading at a rate far beyond what you have been able to do in the past. Be aware of the fact that you are paying excellent attention to the material in part because of the faster speed. Imagine how many more books you will now be able to read. Whenever it feels comfortable for you, take a deep breath, open your eyes, come wide awake. Then get yourself up and with passion, take your next action step.

Attend To Comprehension

Close your eyes, take a deep breath, and imagine your peaceful place. Make this quiet peaceful place you've chosen seem as real as you can. Imagine that you are reading another wonderful book. As you finish, pretend that you are discussing it with someone who has also read it. Be aware of how excellent your comprehension is and how brilliant your recollection is of the material that you read. Imagine how this skill will serve you in the future. Realize the wisdom that could come from all the knowledge you are receiving from all of the brilliant writers you are able to explore. Whenever it feels comfortable for you, take a deep breath, open your eyes, come wide awake. Then get yourself up and with passion, take your next action step.

Best On The Test

Close your eyes, take a deep breath, and imagine your peaceful place. Make this quiet peaceful place you've chosen seem as real as you can. Imagine that you are being tested on something that you have read. Get the feeling that you understood the material perfectly and that you are able not only to remember everything that you read, but also to understand what the author was saying between the lines. You get a sense of the writer's motivation for doing this work, and a feel for the message that was being expressed. This feeling of being an excellent learner combines with the feeling of confidence that you get from performing your best under pressure. Feel that you always do your best when the chips are down, you always remember best when it comes to the test. Whenever it feels comfortable for you, take a deep breath, open your eyes, come wide awake. Then get yourself up and with passion, take your next action step.

Tri-Focus Exercise

Close your eyes, take a deep breath, and imagine your peaceful place. Make this quiet peaceful place you've chosen seem as real as you can. Imagine you are holding your magic book. LOVE THAT BOOK!!! Open the book and see that there are three lines or bars across every line of print.

_____ _____ _____

_____ _____ _____

_____ _____ _____

_____ _____ _____

Allow your eyes to move, left, center, right, left, center, right, across and down the page for a few moments as you continue to LOVE THAT BOOK!!!

Do this tri-focus exercise over and over again and soon it will become an automatic habit. Whenever it feels comfortable for you, take a deep breath, open your eyes, come wide awake. Then get yourself up and with passion, take your next action step.

Creating Prosperity

"Money is interesting," said BrainMind. "It feels like we both love it and hate it at the same time."
    "Money's an energy that carries a charge
    Some have it mastered, for some it's quite large
    They equate it with greed and negative powers
    Insensitive people in white ivory towers

> Some seem to ignore it the best that they can
> It comes in, it goes out, it seems there's no plan
> Whatever they make is whatever they spend
> And next week they go out and do it again
> But some see a force that helps the planet to heal
> It's solid and forceful, undoubtedly real
> If we control it, and dole it with compassion and trust
> Not blame money, for people with hate, greed, and lust," replied
HeartMind.

Jason is a very successful motion picture producer. Over the years, he had made close to forty million dollars. Jason, however, was not prosperous. In fact, he was on the verge of being totally broke. Frivolous spending, risky investments, and two divorces had all but depleted his forty million dollar fortune. Jason is an unhappy man, but a great example of the fact that prosperity is not primarily dependent upon income.

Sarah was a public school teacher for forty-one years. For most of her career, she was making under twenty thousand dollars a year. Her best year was just over twenty-nine thousand. Her total wages (over her life) were about two percent of Jason's income. Sarah, however, is very prosperous. She saved ten percent of every paycheck that she received during those forty-one years. First she invested in regular savings and later in higher paying long term accounts.

When Sarah retired at the age of sixty-five she had one million, seventy-three thousand, one hundred and sixty-seven dollars in her various accounts. Needless to say, Sarah is having a very active retirement. Sarah is another great example that prosperity is not dependent upon income.

Money is a very misunderstood energy form. Most money is not in bills and coins, but instead in electrons floating around in the world's financial computer network. Its relative value is always changing through such things as inflation and recession.

Economics is at best an art form. It would be difficult to call it a science when the world's leading experts always disagree. Relatively few ever master prosperity. Even for many who make a great deal of money, prosperity is no more than an elusive dream. A lot of very wealthy people spend much of their time worrying about money. Most people don't understand even the most basic principle of creating financial prosperity. It is that prosperity is not dependent upon income. Thousands of millionaires have gone bankrupt, and thousands with small incomes continue to become prosperous. People do not create prosperity by increasing their income, for usually that is at least how much money they spend. With increased income for most, comes a higher standard of living, a new car, fancy restaurants, wide screen TV, etc. Prosperity can only be created by saving and investing your money. The key is having the money that comes in make money before it goes back out.

There are three different types of attitudes that people carry about money. There is a small percentage with poverty consciousness, a small percentage with prosperity consciousness, and a very large percentage in the middle, those who have a break-even consciousness.

Poverty consciousness is where there is never enough money, and the bills are always overdue. What needs to go out always seems to be more than what comes in. Generally, if you give a person with a poverty consciousness even a very large sum of money, in a short time it will all be spent on things they consume, or on things that go down in value. They can receive a great deal of money and relatively soon there will be little or nothing to show for it. In fact, it is quite likely that people with poverty consciousness will spend beyond their means and go deeply into debt. People like this can justify almost any expenditure by claiming to have been so long deprived of the luxuries that they previously couldn't afford. Saving and investing are for them completely unknown and unexplored territories. It is an alternative the is so foreign to their lives, it doesn't really even occur to them.

On the other side of the spectrum are those who live their lives in prosperity consciousness, people who handle money effectively and who always have extra money. If you take away from a person with a prosperity consciousness, almost everything he or she owns, it is likely they will rebuild their resources and return quickly to the prosperity that they feel they so richly deserve.

These people do not necessarily have a large income. What prosperous people do is that they save and invest their money, and they make their money grow. Often they invest the majority of their money in safe places, and take risks with the rest.

In between poverty and prosperity is the place where most people live, a place called "break-even" consciousness. Whatever comes in, that's what goes out. However much needs to go out, that's how much comes in. A great month and someone with break-even consciousness will buy something new. A slow month, and somehow their bills get paid. Extra money seems to burn a hole in their pockets. People with break-even consciousness make sure that they do, in fact, break even. If they make a little extra they spend a little extra.

If some emergency happens, somehow they come up with the money. It always works out even, nothing left over at the end of the month. The secret is to save and invest some of your money and to continue to do so on a regular basis.

Here are some ideas about money.

- Track all of the money in your life, what comes in and goes out.
- Save and invest at least ten percent of every single dollar you earn.
- Understand and appreciate what you receive in exchange for money.
- Be generous some of the time and careful always.
- Continue to increase the value of the products or services you offer.
- Set new goals for income, savings and investments, each year.
- Treat your current possessions as if they were very, very valuable.
- Pay all of your bills on time, with a big smile on your face.
- Spend time around prosperous people.

I Pay Myself First

Close your eyes, take a deep breath, and imagine your peaceful place. Make this quiet peaceful place you've chosen seem as real as you can.

106

Imagine that you are receiving payment for the work that you do. Imagine that you are going to the bank to make a deposit into your checking account. After you deposit the money pretend that the first check that you write is for ten percent of that deposit and that you write it to yourself and put it into your savings account. Pretend that you do this every single time. If you find ten dollars on the street, a dollar goes to savings. Imagine that the savings account is growing larger and larger, because you pay yourself first. Enjoy the feelings of increasing prosperity and know you truly deserve it. Whenever it feels comfortable for you, take a deep breath, open your eyes, come wide awake. Then get yourself up and with passion, take your next action step.

Best To Invest

Close your eyes, take a deep breath, and imagine your peaceful place. Make this quiet peaceful place you've chosen seem as real as you can. Imagine that you have been saving ten percent of your income for many, many months and that it is now time to make a major investment. Imagine sitting down with an investment counselor whom you have carefully selected and discussing all of your options. There is a feeling of confidence and security as you realize that your money is about to begin really working for you. Financial security is on the horizon, and it feels wonderful. Feel the sense of confidence and security continue to grow as you leave money problems farther and farther behind you. Whenever it feels comfortable for you, take a deep breath, open your eyes, come wide awake. Then get yourself up and with passion, take your next action step.

Living In Prosperity

Close your eyes, take a deep breath, and imagine your peaceful place. Make this quiet peaceful place you've chosen seem as real as you can. Imagine that you have been effectively saving and investing ten percent of your income for a while now and that it is time to make a major investment in building the dream house that you have always wanted. Imagine working with the designers and the contractors to create this ultimate home. Imagine the builder handing over the keys and the feeling that you get as you take possession of your beautiful new home. Know that this is the best investment that you have ever made, and it will surely continue to increase in value. Thank yourself for taking good care of your money, and know that you always will, and thank yourself for allowing yourself to make this dream come true. Whenever it feels comfortable for you, take a deep breath, open your eyes, come wide awake. Then get yourself up and with passion, take your next action step.

Financial Security

Close your eyes, take a deep breath, and imagine your peaceful place. Make this quiet peaceful place you've chosen seem as real as you can. Imagine that you have been successfully saving and investing your money for a long time now. Imagine how it feels to realize that you now have enough to last you comfortably for the rest of your life, and still your net worth continues to increase. You set a goal of creating life-long financial security, and now, due to prudent investing, you have finally reached it. You are set for life. Imagine sharing this wonderful realization with your loved ones, and notice how proud of you they are. Bask in these feelings of total financial security. Whenever it feels comfortable for you, take a deep breath, open your eyes, come wide awake. Then get yourself up and with passion, take your next action step.

Enhancing Relationships

"Tell me," said BrainMind, "about the relationship between love and freedom."

"The bird alone soaring, is a sign that it's free
As true of a freedom as could ever be
But the lonely bird searches the sky up above,
To join with another, trade freedom for love
For love is not freedom in the sense of alone,
But a freedom much different around love has grown

> Freedom to join, experience, care.
> The freedom of love is the freedom to share
> I want you my lover with all of my heart,
> For freedom feels lonely when we are apart
> I'm free when I'm with you, when all's said and done,
> The truest of freedom is when two are one," replied HeartMind.

William was a wonderful partner in every single way. He and his girlfriend Sheryl had been overjoyed with every single aspect of their relationship. Only now there was a problem. The time was right and they had both started talking about getting married.

This seemed to affect William in a very powerful way. For the first time he started to have second thoughts about the relationship. This was disturbing because he thought that it might mean that he really didn't want to spend his life with Sheryl. He used Alpha to see if that, in fact, was true. William, who was a very auditory person, went into the Alpha state and asked himself the question, "Am I afraid to commit to marrying Sheryl?" The answer came to him instantly. "It's not about Sheryl, the fear is about being married."

When William awoke, he realized that having seen his parents go through a messy divorce he was afraid it would happen to him. He then realized that he was not condemned to repeat their mistakes. His relationship with Sheryl was wonderful and totally different than his Mom and Dad's. With that understanding William and Sheryl joyously started to make plans for their wedding.

When loving is good in a relationship it is usually just one of many areas of focus. But when it is bad, it often becomes an all-consuming problem. Ideally, making love is an Alpha experience. Actually it can be two different Alpha experiences. You are in Alpha when you focus on what you or your partner are experiencing, the physical sensations of the body or the emotional experience of intimacy. You are also in Alpha when you let go and space out into your imagination and fantasy. Imagination and fantasy are very important aspects of the human sexual experience. Not to be ignored is one of the basic functions, to create children. If the purpose of the coupling is procreation, then there is a whole deeper level of communication that happens in the experience. Humans experience sex as more than procreation, but instinctively it is always a factor in our sexual intercourse.

Love in general and lovemaking in particular, provide us with an opportunity to learn about ourselves as we see ourselves reflected in the eyes of our lovers. Each of us teaches our lovers how to love us, through the ways that we love ourselves. We can see our lovers as mirrors for ourselves and in this way better understand who we really are. Enhancing relationships is less a question of technique and more a question of rapport.

Rapport is the connection, the heartfelt communication. Poor technique can be handled through practice if the desire is there. Poor rapport leads to uncomfortable feelings, and poor communication. Relax, tune in and trust your intuition. Pay attention to your partner's gestures and body language. Let communication become more of a loving and learning experience. Be creative, be intuitive, and be open enough to listen to everything that your partner tells you, both in words and in gestures and movements. Romance, in all of it's wondrous forms, can continue to grow through communication and experimentation.

Satisfaction Guaranteed

Close your eyes, take a deep breath, and imagine your peaceful place. Make this quiet peaceful place you've chosen seem as real as you can. Imagine that you have just finished making warm, tender, passionate love with that special someone in your life. Get in touch with the sensations inside your body, the calmness, the relaxation, the warm glow inside your heart. Now focus on the external sensations, the natural scent of your lover, and the way it feels with your lover next to you. Get in touch with the bonding, the connection that making love has helped to create. Feel a sense of oneness with your lover, stronger than you have ever felt it before. Feel a deep sense of satisfaction, a sense of togetherness that goes far beyond the physical closeness. Whenever it feels comfortable for you, take a deep breath, open your eyes, come wide awake. Then get yourself up and with passion, take your next action step.

Beforeplay

Close your eyes, take a deep breath, and imagine your peaceful place. Make this quiet peaceful place you've chosen seem as real as you can. Imagine yourself standing and facing your lover just prior to making love. Look into your lover's eyes and see the passion that is stirring there. Look deep into the eyes of your lover and thereby deep into your lover's soul. As your lover looks deep into you, begin to feel a similar feeling of passion stirring inside yourself that enhances the sense of connection that flows between you. Let this feeling of oneness, of synergy, begin to build and build, even before you reach out to each other. Tune into this wonderful feeling. Whenever it feels comfortable for you, take a deep breath, open your eyes, come wide awake. Then get yourself up and with passion, take your next action step

Loving Compliments

Close your eyes, take a deep breath, and imagine your peaceful place. Make this quiet peaceful place you've chosen seem as real as you can. Imagine that in a non-sexual setting, your partner is complimenting you on what a wonderful lover you are. Listen to the comments about passion and consideration. Listen to the comments about excitement and creativity. Enjoy the feelings that these compliments evoke in you. Know that they are richly deserved. Now take this opportunity to express back to your lover just what her or his words have meant to you, and how important it was to you that they were shared. Feel a sense of pride and confidence growing deep inside you. Whenever it feels comfortable for you, take a deep breath, open your eyes, come wide awake. Then get yourself up and with passion, take your next action step.

Totally Tactile

Close your eyes, take a deep breath, and imagine your peaceful place. Make this quiet peaceful place you've chosen seem as real as you can.

Imagine that you are in bed with your lover. Imagine that all of the tactile receptor sites in your body and especially on the surface of your skin are gently becoming more and more sensitive. Feel intensely the sensation of your lover's caress. Notice the enhanced sensation in your own fingertips as you return the caress. As more of your skin comes in contact with your lover's skin, feel yourself let go and fully experience the sensations which accompany this enhanced sensitivity. Watch how your lover enjoys it too. Notice a form of communication between the two of you that goes far beyond words. Whenever it feels comfortable for you, take a deep breath, open your eyes, come wide awake. Then get yourself up and with passion, take your next action step.

Quotes *to* Grow By

"People become really quite remarkable when they start thinking that they can do things. When they believe in themselves they have the first secret of success."

Dr. Norman Vincent Peale
1898-1993, Speaker and Author

"I learned this, at least, by my experiment; that if one advances confidently in the direction of his dreams, and endeavors to live the life which he has imagined, he will meet with a success unexpected in common hours."

Henry David Thoreau
1817-1862, Writer and Poet

"Man often becomes what he believes himself to be. If I keep on saying to myself that I cannot do a certain thing, it is possible that I may end by really becoming incapable of doing it. On the contrary, if I have the belief that I can do it, I shall surely acquire the capacity to do it even if I may not have it at the beginning."

Mahatma Gandhi
1869-1948, Indian Political Leader

"The difference between the impossible and the possible lies in a man's determination.

Tommy Lasorda
1927, "Hall of Fame" Baseball Manager

"The only thing that stands between a man and what he wants from life is often merely the will to try it and the faith to believe that it is possible."

David Viscott
1938-1996, Psychiatrist and Author

"A great attitude does much more than turn on the lights in our worlds; it seems to magically connect us to all sorts of serendipitous opportunities that were somehow absent before the change."

Earl Nightingale

1921-1989, Philosopher and Syndicated Radio Personality

"One of the secrets of success is to refuse to let temporary setbacks defeat us."

Mary Kay

1918-2001, Founder of Mary Kay Cosmetics

"We can let circumstances rule us, or we can take charge and rule our lives from within."

Earl Nightingale

1921-1989, Philosopher and Syndicated Radio Personality

"We are what we repeatedly do. Excellence, then, is not an act, but a habit."

Aristotle

384-322 BC, Greek Philosopher and Scientist

"The victory of success is half won when one gains the habit of setting goals and achieving them. Even the most tedious chore will become endurable as you parade through each day convinced that every task, no matter how menial or boring, brings you closer to fulfilling your dreams."

Og Mandino

1923-1996, Author and Speaker

"Opportunity does not just come along—it is there all the time—we just have to see it."

Earl Nightingale

1921-1989, Philosopher and Syndicated Radio Personality

"Formulate and stamp indelibly on your mind a mental picture of your-self succeeding. Hold this picture tenaciously. Never permit it to fade. Your mind will seek to develop the picture . . . Do not build up obsta-cles in your imagination."

Dr. Norman Vincent Peale
1898-1993, Speaker and Author

"If you really want something, and really work hard, and take advantage of opportunities, and never give up, you will find a way. "

Jane Goodall
1934, Scientist and UN Messenger of Peace

"If you don't like something, change it. If you can't change it, change your attitude."

Maya Angelou
1928-2014, Author and Poet

"If you accept a limiting belief, then it will become a truth for you."

Louise Hay
1926, Author and Speaker

"There is no passion to be found playing small—in settling for a life that is less than the one you are capable of living."

Nelson Mandela
1918-2013, Former Prime Minister of South Africa

"Even a mistake may turn out to be the one thing necessary to a worthwhile achievement."

Henry Ford
1863-1947, American Industrialist

"Every now and then a man's mind is stretched by a new idea or sensation, and never shrinks back to its former dimensions."

Oliver Wendell Holmes Sr.

1809-1894, Author

"It's kind of fun to do the impossible."

Walt Disney

1901-1966, Entertainment Innovator

"Keep away from people who try to belittle your ambitions. Small people always do that, but the really great make you feel that you, too, can become great."

Mark Twain

1835-1910, Writer and Humorist

"I make the most of all that comes and the least of all that goes."

Sara Teasdale

1884-1933, Poet

"Every memorable act in the history of the world is a triumph of enthusiasm. Nothing great was ever achieved without it because it gives any challenge or any occupation, no matter how frightening or difficult, a new meaning. Without enthusiasm you are doomed to a life of mediocrity but with it you can accomplish miracles."

Og Mandino

1923-1996, Author and Speaker

"Those who love deeply never grow old; they may die of old age, but they die young."

Benjamin Franklin

1706-1790, Scientist, Publisher and Diplomat

"Most of the important things in the world have been accomplished by people who have kept on trying when there seemed to be no help at all."

Dale Carnegie
1888-1955, Author and Trainer

"With ordinary talent and extraordinary perseverance, all things are attainable."

Sir Thomas Fowell Buxton, 1st Baronet
1786-1846, Abolitionist and Social Reformer

"As long as you keep a person down, some part of you has to be down there to hold him down, so it means you cannot soar as you otherwise might."

Marian Anderson
1897-1993, Opera Singer

"What we see depends mainly on what we look for."

Sir John Lubbock, 1st Baronet Avebury
1834-1913, British Statesman and Naturalist

"Look at a day when you are supremely satisfied at the end. It's not a day when you lounge around doing nothing; it's when you've had everything to do, and you've done it."

Margaret Thatcher
1925-2013, Former British Prime Minister

"I know for sure that what we dwell on is who we become. . . . Become the change you want to see—those are words I live by."

Oprah Winfrey
1954, Media Personality

"I never could have done what I have done without the habits of punctuality, order, and diligence, without the determination to concentrate myself on one subject at a time."

Charles Dickens

1812-1870, Writer

"The best way to predict the future is to invent it."

Alan Kay

1940, Computer Scientist

"The young do not know enough to be prudent, and therefore they attempt the impossible—and achieve it, generation after generation."

Pearl S. Buck

1892-1973, Author, Nobel and Pulitzer Prize Winner

"The person interested in success has to learn to view failure as a healthy, inevitable part of the process of getting to the top."

Dr. Joyce Brothers

1927-2013, Psychologist and Television Personality

"Pain is temporary, it may last a minute, or an hour, or a day, or a year, but eventually it will subside and something else will take its place. If I quit, however, it lasts forever."

Lance Armstrong

1971, Athlete

"Whatever you vividly imagine, ardently desire, sincerely believe, and enthusiastically act upon . . . must inevitably come to pass!"

Paul J. Meyer

1928-2009, Writer

"The tragedy of life doesn't lie in not reaching your goal. The tragedy lies in having no goal to reach."

Benjamin Mays

1894-1984, Educator and Minister

"The bottom line in any area of life is cause and effect," said Brain-Mind. "Imagining that I can see, or hear, or feel we have what we want, lets you add the passion or love to set it into motion.

It was The Beatles last lines, for Heaven's sake, where they said, '. . . in the end, the love you take, is equal to the love you make.'"

My Favorite Books *and* Authors

Siddhartha
and other works by
Hermann Hesse

Night
and other works by
Elie Wiesel

Hamlet
and other works by
William Shakespeare

Huckleberry Finn
and other works by
Mark Twain

Time Enough For Love
and other works by
Robert A. Heinlein

Illusions
and other works by
Richard Bach

The Sherlock Holmes Series
Sir Arthur Conan Doyle

The Foundation Trilogy
and other works by
Issac Asimov

The Power of Positive Thinking
and other works by
Dr. Norman Vincent Peale

The Art of Loving
and other works by
Eric Fromm

As a Man Thinketh
James Allen

Chicken Soup for the Soul Books
Jack Canfield, Mark Victor
Hansen

Mindfulness
Ellen J. Langer

Wherever You Go, There You Are
and other works by
Jon Kabat-Zinn

Drive
and other works by
Daniel H. Pink

Man's Search for Meaning
and other works by
Viktor E. Frankl

Think and Grow Rich
and other works by
Napoleon Hill

Psycho-Cybernetics
Maxwell Maltz

Be Here Now
and other works by
Baba Ram Dass

*How To Win Friends And
Influence People*
and other works by
Dale Carnegie

Brave New World
and other works by
Aldous Huxley

The Practice Effect
and other works by
David Brin

Way Of The Peaceful Warrior
and other works by
Dan Millman

The Relaxation Response
Herbert Benson, M.D.

Man and His Symbols
and other works by
Carl Gustav Jung

Love is Letting Go of Fear
and other works by
Gerald G. Jampolski, M.D.

The Dragon Doesn't Live Here Anymore
Alan Cohen

Flow
Mihaly Csikszentmihalyi

Zen Mind, Beginner's Mind
Shunryu Suzuki

The Signal and the Noise
Nate Silver

Fooling Houdini
Alex Stone

A Primer in Positive Psychology
Christopher Peterson

A Return to Love
and other works by
Maryann Williamson

The Magic of Believing
Claude M. Bristol

Awaken the Giant Within
and other works by
Anthony Robbins

Exploring the World of Lucid Dreaming
Stephen LaBerge

The Dream Book
Betty Bethards

The Power of Now
and other works by
Eckhart Tolle

The Silva Mind Control Method
Jose Silva

Seth Speaks
and other works by
Jane Roberts

The Varieties of Religious Experience
and other works by
William James

A Course in Miracles (Combined Volume)
Foundation for Inner Peace

The Aquarian Conspiracy
Marilyn Ferguson

The Power of Myth
and other works by
Joseph Campbell

The Richest Man in Babylon
George S. Clason

The Greatest Salesman in the World
Og Mandino

Authentic Happiness
and other works by
Martin E. P. Seligman

The Dancing Wu Li Masters
and other works by
Gary Zukov

The Tao of Physics
and other works by
Frijof Capra

The Prophet
Kahlil Gibran

The Art of War
Sun Tzu

Frogs Into Princes
and other works by
Richard Bandler, John Grinder

My Voice Will Go With You
Sidney Rosen

The Charge
Brendon Burchard

Multiple Intelligences
and other works by
Howard E. Gardner

Getting Well Again
and other works by
O. Carl Simonton, M.D.

Autobiography of a Yogi
Paramahansa Yogananda

Altered States of Consciousness
and other works by
Charles T. Tart

Emotional Intelligence
and other works by
Daniel Goleman

The 7 Habits of Highly Successful People
and other works by
Stephen R. Covey

The Wisdom of the Enneagram
and other works by
Don Richard Riso, Russ Hudson

The Enneagram in Love and Work
and other works by
Helen Palmer

They Call Me Coach
and other works by
John Wooden

The Three Pillars of Zen
Roshi P. Kapleau

Creative Visualization
Shakti Gawain

On Death and Dying
and other works by
Elisabeth Kübler-Ross

Crack in the Cosmic Egg
and other works by
Joseph Chilton Pearce

When Bad Things Happen to Good People
and other works by
Harold S. Kushner

The Essential Rumi
Coleman Barks

Leaves of Grass
Walt Whitman

Boom! Voices of the Sixties
Tom Brokaw

The Fabric of the Cosmos
and other works by
Brian Greene

The great thinkers
Rupert Lodge

One Minute Manager
and other works by
Kenneth Blanchard, PhD

Influencing With Integrity
Jeanne Z.

Good to Great
and other works by
Jim Collins

Non-Violent Resistance
and other works by
Mohandas K. Gandhi

The World is Flat
and other works by
Thomas L. Friedman

The Five Love Languages
and other works by
Gary D. Chapman

David and Goliath
and other works by
Malcolm Gladwell

Getting Things Done
and other works by
David Allen

You Can Heal Your Life
and other works by
Louise L. Hay

The Art of Happiness
and other works by
Dalai Lama

Seven Spiritual Laws of Success
and other works by
Deepak Chopra

Why We Buy
Paco Underhill

Ungifted
Scott Barry Kaufman

Huey
David Groen, Jay Groen

*Roll Me Up and Smoke Me a
When I Die*
Willie Nelson, Kinky Friedman

Healing Back Pain
John E. Sarno

Who I Am
Pete Townsend

Waging Heavy Peace
Neil Young

Cronkite
Douglas Brinkley

Last Words
and other works by
George Carlin

Truman
and other works by
David McCullough

My Mother Was Nuts
Penny Marshall

Telegraph Avenue
and other works by
Michael Chabon

New York
and other works by
Edward Rutherfurd

2030
Albert Brooks

Mad Mouse
and other works by
Chris Grabenstein

*The Man Who Mistook His Wife
for a Hat*
Oliver Sacks

Fierce Conversations
Susan Scott

Making a Good Brain Great
Daniel G. Amen, MD

The Nero Wolfe Series
Rex Stout

The Travis McGee Series
and other works by
John D. MacDonald

*The Peter Decker & Rina Lazarus
Novels*
and other works by
Faye Kellerman

The Alex Delaware Novels
and other works by
Jonathan Kellerman

*The Kinsey Millhone Alphabet
Mysteries*
Sue Grafton

The Spencer Series
and other works by
Robert B. Parker

The Martian Chronicles
and other works by
Ray Bradbury

To Kill a Mocking Bird
Harper Lee

1984
George Orwell

Lord of the Flies
and other works by
William Golding

One Flew Over the Cuckoo's Nest
and other works by
Ken Kesey

The Sun Also Rises
and other works by
Ernest Hemingway

Invisible Man
Ralph Ellison

Ragtime
and other works by
E. L. Doctorow

Portnoy's Complaint
and other works by
Philip Roth

Rabbit Run
and other works by
John Updike

The Painted Bird
and other works by
Jerry Kosinski

On The Road
Jack Kerouac

Never Go Back
and other works by
Lee Child

Gone Girl
Gillian Flynn

The Dirk Pitt Adventures
and other works by
Clive Cussler

Slaughterhouse-Five
and other works by
Kurt Vonnegut

The Harry Potter Series
J. K. Rowling

Childhood's End
and other works by
Arthur C. Clarke

2150 A.D.
Thea Plym Alexander

The Client
and other works by
John Grisham

The Metamorphosis
and other works by
Franz Kafka

Catcher in the Rye
and other works by
J. D. Salinger

Great Expectations
and other works by
Charles Dickens

Hit Man
and other works by
Lawrence Block

The Last Bookstore in America
Amy Stewart

Extremely Loud and Incredibly Close
Jonathan Safran Foer

Murder on the Orient Express
and other works by
Agatha Christie

The Mote in God's Eye
and other works by
Larry Niven, Jerry Pournelle

The Hit
and other works by
David Balducci

The Spellman Files
and other works by
Lisa Lutz

The Silent Hour
and other works by
Michael Koryta

Sleep No More
and other works by
Iris Johansen

Rules of Crime
and other works by
L. J. Sellers

Six Years
and other works by
Harlan Coben

Mr. Penumbra's 24-Hour Bookstore
Robin Sloan

Time Travel Adventures of The 1800 Club (1-9)
Robert McAuley

Found
and other works by
H. Terrell Griffin

The Sacketts Series
and other works by
Louis L'Amour

Standup Guy
and other works by
Stuart Woods

Cross My Heart
and other works by
James Patterson

Hostage
and other works by
Kay Hooper

The Goldfinch
Donna Tartt

The a Gods of Guilt
and other works by
Michael Connelly

The Education of Little Tree
Forrest Carter

Paper Towns
and other works by
John Green

Trout Fishing in America
and other works by
Richard Brautigan

Jurassic Park
and other works by
Michael Crichton

For Whom the Bell Tolls
and other works by
Ernest Hemingway

Lincoln
and other works by
Gore Vidal

Tuesdays with Morrie
and other works by
Mitch Albom

The Martian: A Novel
Andy Weir

The Fault in Our Stars
and other works by
John Green

New York
Edward Rutherford

Excellence in Teaching and Learning
Barbara K. Given & Bobbie
DePorter

Zen Mind, Beginner's Mind
Shunryu Suzuki

*Into the Magic Shop: A
Neurosurgeon's Quest to Discover
the Mysteries of the Brain and the
Secrets of the Heart*
James R. Doty MD

The Mindfulness Solution
Ronald D. Siegel

*Happiness: A Guide to Developing
Life's Most Important Skill*
Matthieu Ricard

*Most Likely To Succeed: Preparing
our Kids for the Innovation
Era* Tony Wagner & Ted
Dintersmith

*Sapient: A Brief History of
Humankind*
Yuval Noah Harari

*The Feeling Brain: The Biology and
Psychology of Emotions* Elizabeth
Johnston & Leah Olson

*Thinking: The New Science of
Decision-Making, Problem-Solving,
and Prediction*
John Brockman

*Search Inside Yourself: The
Unexpected Path to Achieving
Success, Happiness (and World
Peace)*
Chase- Meng Tan

Raising Kids Who Read
Daniel T. Willingham

127

Mindful Work: How Meditation is Changing Business from the Inside Out
David Gelles

Quantum Warrior: The Future of the Mind
John Kehoe

Retire! Don't Retire
Ken Blanchard & Morton Shaevitz

The Psychology of Emotions, Feelings and Thoughts
Mark Pettinelli

Mindwise: Why We Misunderstand What Others Think, Believe, Feel, and Want
Nicholas Epley

Doubt: A History
Jennifer Michael Hecht

Why We Make Mistakes
Joseph T. Hallinan

Why Everyone (Else) Is a Hypocrite
Robert Kurzban

I Can See Clearly Now
Dr. Wayne W. Dyer

The Future of the Mind
Michio Kaku

Focus: The Hidden Driver of Excellence
Daniel Goleman

The History of New Thought
John S. Haller, Jr.

Free Will
Sam Harris

The Fifties
David Halberstam

The Moral Molecule: How Trust Works
Paul J. Zak

Reading in the Brain
Stanislas Dehaene

Fooling Houdini
Alex Stone

Imagine: How Creativity Works
Jonah Lehrer

The Connected Educator
Sheryl Nussbaum-Beach & Lani Ritter Hall

Just One Thing
Rick Hanson PhD

The Miracle of Mindfulness
Thick Nhat Hanh, Vo-Dihn Mai & Mobi Ho

Thoughts Without a Thinker
Mark Epstein

Wherever You Go, There You Are
Jon Kabat-Zinn

Drive
Daniel Pink

Testimony
Robbie Robertson

Born to Run
Bruce Springsteen

Who I Am
Pete Townshend

A Natural Woman
Carole King

Wild Tales
Graham Nash

Even This I Get to Experience
Norman Lear

About the Author

Steven Snyder was a most unusual kid and grew up to be a most unusual man who has literally changed the lives of tens of thousands of people. For starters:

By the time he was three, Steve was reading a book a day. In first grade, his teacher asked the class if anyone already knew how to read. He was the only one who raised his hand. "How many books have you read, Steven?" she quizzed. "About 1,400," Steven answered quite innocently. Did she believe him? Only after he named about a dozen titles of which he knew the plots. Did the woman faint? Her knees probably went a bit weak. What would she do with him while she taught her class to read? Guess what. She literally put him in the corner. He was punished for knowing how to read.

This happened in the Los Angeles area where he was born and lived with his mother and father and his grandmother and uncle. "Four parents instead of two," he smiles. When he was almost three, they moved to the San Fernando Valley and his only sibling, a brother, was born.

When Steve was eight, he learned about self-hypnosis and was introduced to the concept of altered states of consciousness. He was instantly fascinated, and it quickly became his hobby. He began to read everything that he could find on any inter-related topic.

When Steve was 12, his Father left. He left suddenly; never saying good-bye, and Steve never heard from him again . . . another amazing impact of the darkest kind. "Dealing with my fears of abandonment I spent many years both in and out of therapy searching my soul for the lessons that this experience offered," he admits. "And, as painful as it has been, it has at least been as valuable as an agent for growth and change."

Then one night, later that year, he woke up from a dream that suggested he take his two hobbies, reading and self-hypnosis, and do them at the same time. Over the following three years, he created and developed a unique teaching program, HypnoReading, which transformed his life. He started by teaching his friends and then the day after his fifteenth birthday, on January 6, 1967 he began teaching his first class for money. He has been teaching professionally ever since.

In 1978, Steven co-founded Live and Learn, a non-profit 501(c)(3) Educational Foundation in Sherman Oaks, California. Staffed by 15 to 20 employees, the Foundation's focus was to teach enhanced living and accelerated learning skills through counseling, workshops, and seminars to people (especially school teachers) interested in maximizing their potential. Successful fund raising allowed them to provide scholarships. "Live and Learn's corporate mission," Steve explains, "was to help facilitate the gentle overthrow of the school system and to assist society's transition into a system of 21st Century Information Age Education."

In 1987, Steven began doing corporate seminars and by 1991 was in such great demand that he closed Live and Learn to focus on his corporate work. In 1988, he began working with the Young Presidents' Organization (YPO) and in 1990 he began his association with TEC: The Executive Committee. A highly valued speaker for TEC, now Vistage International, the word's largest CEO organization, Steve has presented to over 1,100 groups and was chosen in 2003 as their International Speaker of the Year and in 2012 was honored with the Lifetime Achievement Award.

Along with Michael Benner he hosted the Breakthrough Radio Show, created a series of Breakthrough Audio Journeys on CD, and conducted the life enhancing Breakthrough Seminars. Steve and Michael's work together has evolved into a weekly podcast, "Finding yourself in Paradise." They have a website at www.FocusedPassion.com.

Steve sits on the Board of Directors of Learning Forum International, who along with QLN and SuperCamp have integrated Steve's accelerated reading and learning methods into the programs and trainings that they present to students and teachers world-wide.

Steven was married (in 1999 for the first and only time) to Teresa Allred. A beautiful and accomplished woman, Teresa was the co-owner and CEO of Ontic Engineering and Manufacturing Inc., the nation's largest licensed manufacturer of aircraft parts. Teresa and her brother sold their business and retired in 2006. Steve and Teresa now spend most of their time together with their two Golden Retrievers, Kula and Kili, and their two cats Mango and Guava, in paradise, developing their tropical fruit orchard on seventy acres on a cliff overlooking the ocean in Lower Nahiku, on the beautiful island of Maui.

Contact Steven Snyder

www.FocusedPassion.com
www.snyderisms.com
www.focusedpassionthebook.com

steven.snyder@mac.com

P. O. Box 580 Hana, HI 96713
(808) 268-7558

Seminars Around The World

Abu Dhabi, Adelaide, Agra, Akron, Albany, Amsterdam, Anchorage, Antalya, Aspen, Athens, Atlanta, Auckland, Austin, Baltimore, Bangkok, Bangor, Barcelona, Birmingham, Bogota, Bombay, Bonn, Boston, Brisbane, Bristol, British West Indies, Brussels, Budapest, Buenos Aries, Calgary, Cape Town, Caracas, Carmel, Charleston, Chicago, Charlotte, Cleveland, Columbus, Colorado Springs, Coolum, Costa Mesa, Dallas, Darwin, Delhi, Denver, Detroit, Dubai, Dublin, Durbin, Edinburgh, Edmonton, El Paso, Fort Worth, Geneva, Guatemala City, The Hague, Hamburg, Hana, Hermosa Beach, Hilo, Hong Kong, Honolulu, Hood River, Houston, Indianapolis, Irvine, Issaquah, Istanbul, Johannesburg, Kahului, Kansas City, Krakow, Kuala Lumpur, Lagos, Lahaina, La Paz, Las Vegas, Lexington, Lima, Little Rock, London, Long Island, Los Altos, Los Angeles, Louisville, Madrid, Manchester, Manila, Malibu, Mauritius, Melbourne, Memphis, Mexicali, Mexico City, Miami, Milwaukee, Minneapolis, Mission Viejo, Monterey, Monterrey, Montreal, Mountain View, Nahiku, Nashville, New Jersey, New Orleans, New York, Nottingham, Oakland, Oceanside, Oklahoma City, Omaha, Ontario, Orlando, Oslo, Ottawa, Panama City, Paris, Pasadena, Perth, Philadelphia, Phoenix, Pittsburgh, Playa Del Rey, Plymouth, Portland, Quebec, Queensland, Queenstown, Quito, Raleigh, Rapid City, Redding, Redondo Beach, Reno, Rio de Janeiro, Sacramento, St. Bart, St. Kitts, St.Louis, St. Nevis, St. John, Salt Lake City, Salzburg, San Antonio, San Bernardino, San Diego, San Francisco, San Jose, San Juan, San Salvador, Santa Barbara, Santa Clara, Santa Cruz, Santa Fe, San Francisco, Santa Monica, Santiago, Santo Domingo, Sao Paulo, Scottsdale, Seattle, Shanghai, Singapore, Springfield, Stamford, Stockholm, Sydney, Taipei, Tampa, Tokyo, Toledo, Toronto, Tucson, Tulsa, Vancouver, Victoria, Vienna, Winnipeg, Washington D.C.

Made in the
USA
Columbia, SC